City Travel Kit

SEVEN DAYS IN PARIS

Published by Doubleday
a division of Bantam Doubleday Dell Publishing Group, Inc
666 Fifth Avenue, New York, New York 10103

Doubleday and the portrayal of an anchor with a dolphin are trademarks of
Doubleday, a division of Bantam Doubleday Dell Publishing Group, Inc

Library of Congress Cataloging-in-Publication Data
Halden, William.
    City Travel Kit, Paris/ William Halden and Carole Halden -- 1st ed.
      p.   cm.
    ISBN 0-385-26173-X
    1. Paris (France) -- Description -- 1975 - -- Guide-books. 2. Paris
    (France) -- Description -- 1975 - -- Tours. I. Halden, Carole.
    DC708.H26 1990   89-35033
    914.4'3604838 -- dc20   CIP

ISBN 0-385-26173-X
Copyright © 1990 Carole and William Halden
April 1990
First Edition

Originally published in Great Britain by
Webb & Bower (Publishers) Limited
5 Cathedral Close, Exeter, Devon EX1 1EZ

Seven Days in Paris
was edited and designed by the
William Halden Organization
Cover and design concept Carole Thomas Associates
Picture editing One Way Design
Editorial assistance Diane Goldby
Colour reproduction Peninsular Repro Services, Exeter, England
Printed and bound New Interlitho SpA, Milan, Italy

CITY TRAVEL KIT

SEVEN · DAYS · IN
Paris

by

Carole and William Halden

Doubleday

New York   London   Toronto   Sydney   Auckland

introducing ...

... **Seven Days in Paris**, a new concept in guidebooks.
From the first morning of waking in this dazzling city, the book
takes over. First, it presents a theme for each day whether
the visit is one, two or seven days. Then it introduces,
smoothly and without fuss, the treasures and splendours of
the city. There is no need to struggle with complicated
symbols, confusing opening times, tortuous explanations
and endless history.

The text gives easy-to-understand directions, picks out in
bold type the sights really worth seeing - and explains why.
The sequence of tours can begin on any day. Avoid the
theme of *Shopping in Style* on a Sunday and *Art and artists*
on a Monday or Tuesday - many museums close on one of
those days.

Finally, each part of every day is timed and the only
interruptions are directions to the city's most delightful and
welcoming restaurants for coffee, lunch, tea and dinner. At
the end of the stay, this guide will have made sure that the
very best of Paris has been seen, enjoyed and appreciated.

contributors

Madeleine and Douglas Johnson who wrote the section *People and Places* are authors of *The Age of Illusion: Art and Politics in France between the Wars*. Douglas Johnson is Professor of French History at University College, London, and the author of several other books. His French-born wife Madeleine was formerly Head of Modern Languages at St Paul's School for Girls in London.

David Loftus, creator of the collage on the cover, has shown at the Illustrators' Gallery and the Best of British Illustration Exhibition.

Michael Munday whose watercolour maps illustrate the itineraries is chairman of the Board of Governors of the Association of Illustrators.

Jennie Pearson, the illustrator for *People and Places*, was Resident Designer at Fremantle Art Centre, Perth, Western Australia.

the authors also wish to thank

Dr Adriano Agnati, Director, Dr Roberto Melis,
Annamaria Mannucci and Fiorenza Frigoni, Touring Club Italiano
Valérie Coat, Maison de la France
Pauline Hallam, French Government Tourist Office, London
Jean Larue, La Tour Eiffel
Marie José Mercier, Musée National du Château de Versailles
Patricia Mounier, Musée du Louvre
Véronica O'Connor, Paris Vision
Hélène Padovani, Acoustiguide

and for pictures used in this book

Maison de la France, Paris and French Government Tourist Office,
London, except: pages 11 & 64 Richard Passmore, Colorific!; pages
15, 16, 17, 34, 40/41, 42, 43 & 55 Réunion des Musées Nationaux;
page 22 Morabito; page 23-top Peter Tenzer, Colorific!; page 39 Bruno
Jarret, Musée Rodin; page 46/47 David Moore, Colorific!; and pages
59 & 63 Jean Paul Nacivet, Colorific!

contents

Patterns of Paris

Climb the Arc de Triomphe, stroll along the Champs-Élysées past the fashion couturiers of Avenue Georges V and board the bus for the sights of Paris

Paris has to be experienced not just visited. The city *is* beautiful and Parisians will always say it is the *most* beautiful in the world, but its attraction eludes description.

Today begins that experience by strolling along the boulevards, sitting at pavement cafés and then, with a guided bus tour, fitting the landmarks into place.

Start at métro station *Charles de Gaulle, Étoile*. Outside is the **Arc de Triomphe**, the national symbol of unity. It stands in the centre of Étoile which, worthy of its name, is a star-shaped junction from which twelve wide avenues radiate.

A first impression of the arch's vastness can be gained by viewing it from the safety of the pavements around the Place de l'Étoile. Each

of the hundreds of seemingly tiny figures on the frieze around the arch is two metres tall. Of the four sculpture groups at the base of the pillars *Départ des Volontaires de 1729* or *La Marseillaise* which is on the right side facing the Champs-Élysées is the only one with verve and inspiration. It was unfortunate that its sculptor, Rude, was pushed into the background by the jealousy and scheming of other artists, for this is the high point of the decoration of the monument.

Use one of the two pedestrian underpasses, solemn in marble and bronze, to reach the arch. The entrances are on either side of the arch, one at the top of the Champs-Élysées, to the right looking at the arch, the other at the top of the

6

Avenue de la Grande Armée. The tunnels emerge close to the flame of remembrance to the Unknown Soldier. Buy an elevator ticket or walk up the 284 steps and at the top is the viewing terrace.

From here, fifty metres above the traffic, can be seen landmarks of the city's past: Notre-Dame, the Louvre and the full length of Avenue des Champs-Élysées. In the other direction is its future: skyscrapers of the new business district La Défense with its showcase, the Grande Arche.

Leave the Arc de Triomphe by the underpass for the **Champs-Élysées** and set off down the avenue on the shady, right-hand side to the Office de Tourisme at No 127. Although reservations can be made direct, this is a good opportunity to book this afternoon's sightseeing (Discovery Tour, Paris Vision), Day Two's visit to the Moulin Rouge (Paris Vision), and Day Seven's dinner-cruise on the river Seine (Bateaux-Mouches). Also pick up a five-day bargain *carte*

musées, the pass into over sixty of the city's museums - an extra benefit is that it helps avoid queues.

Next door to the tourist office is the famous Drugstore, open until the early hours, with everything from groceries to books alongside the pharmacy.

Continue along the avenue. On both sides, prestige banks, airlines, and luxury car manufacturers mingle with the pavement cafés, shopping malls and cinemas.

COFFEE: After a few hundred metres, on the corner with Avenue George V, is Fouquets, one-time haunt of Art Buchwald and international journalists, now the favourite of French cinema and showbiz stars. Plenty of bustle and although expensive for a coffee or beer it is the café from which to see the world go by.

Next an opportunity to add a little *je ne sais quoi* to the wardrobe. Turn down **Avenue George V** and 7

into **Rue François 1er** to see what the opulent and famous will be wearing this season. Ted Lapidus is at No 35 and Pierre Balmain at No 44. Walk back into Avenue George V by turning right along Rue Marbeuf. Across the avenue, slightly to the right, is the **American Cathedral**. Just inside the door can be seen the cloistered Dean's Garden and, to the right, the century-old Episcopal church with its Gothic-style architecture. The notice-board reports on the lively activities of the congregation of three hundred Americans in varied occupations from diplomacy to language teaching.

Turn right on leaving and at the far end of the avenue by the bridge Pont de l'Alma, is Givenchy. Ready-to-wear outfits can be admired in the elegant ground-floor showroom while upstairs is the hallowed ground of the *haute couture* salon.

Outside, turn left along the **Avenue Montaigne** and after crossing Rue François 1er is Christian Dior. Nina Ricci is at No 39 and the lovely Japanese silks of Hanae Mori at No 17.

Paris is the capital of *haute couture* and the fashion weeks in February and July, when the houses show their collections to the world's press, are internationally famous. These are filmed on video to be shown to prospective customers. Tickets for these viewings can be obtained by direct approach to the couturiers' showrooms or through hotel reception desks.

Continue on, back into Champs-Élysées and the **Rond Point des Champs-Élysées**. The 19th century fountain in the centre was redesigned in 1958 and split into six to speed the traffic. On the corner of Avenue Montaigne behind wrought ironwork grilles, is **Hôtel de Lehon**, the only building left of the original splendour of Champs-Élysées. It belonged to Countess de Lehon, mistress of the Duc de Morny. To be close to her the duke had a small mansion built nearby at No 15 and this became known as *La niche de Fidèle*, Fido's kennel.

Cross the avenue towards the façade of what used to be the offices of the Paris daily newspaper *Le Figaro*. At No 12 is **St Laurent Rive Gauche** boutique, the ritziest of the Paris couturiers. Off the street is **Galerie Élysées**, bright and noisy in the style of shopping malls that first started on this side of the avenue and have spread into shopping streets the world over. Escalators and fountains with shops selling everything from clothes to confectionary, jewellery to gadgets.

Outside, walk along the Champs-Élysées in the direction of Place de la Concorde with, on the far side, the **Grand Palais** and **Petit Palais**, built for the Exhibition of 1900. The Petit Palais is now the Museum of Fine Arts and the Grand Palais, with its Ionic colonnade and glass dome, houses art exhibitions and book fairs.

This stretch of the Champs-Élysées, is so different from the bustling commercial and tourist-thronged section. The gardens and overhanging trees, together with the sandy spaces - now rarely dog-defiled, thanks to green-clad *Propreté de Paris* crews equipped with mobile vacuum cleaners - are where Parisians play *pétanque* with metal *boules*.

Into **Place de la Concorde** which, night or day, sunrise or particularly at sunset, is one of the loveliest open squares in the world.

Here, in 1763, the merchants and worthy aldermen of Paris erected a plinth with an equestrian statue of Louis XV, in the new square especially designed for it. People were not quite so royalist as they had been under the 72-year reign of his father Louis XIV and they hung a placard around the neck of the horse: *What a lovely statue, what a lovely plinth. All the Virtues walk, whilst Vice rides.* The royal statue was enthusiastically toppled in the Revolution.

Cross to the **obelisk** in the centre which was donated in 1829 by Mehemet Ali, Viceroy of Egypt, in gratitude for help from France, and in anticipation of more. Two other famous obelisks, *Cleopatra's Needle* in London and one in New York's Central Park, were given for similar reasons. From the pedestal

8

Arc de Triomphe: dominating the Champs-Élysées

9

are spectacular views of the Pont de la Concorde, Champs-Élysées, La Madeleine and the Louvre. On either side are the **fountains,** inspired by those in St Peter's Square, Rome and around the edges of the square, on **Gabriel** pedestals, are eight female figures representing provincial cities. *Lille* and *Strasbourg* are by **Pradier**.

Leave the obelisk, and cross to **Jardin des Tuileries**. Designed by Le Nôtre, as were the gardens at Versailles and Vaux-le-Vicomte, they set a pattern for formal landscaping that has not been equalled.

It was from here that Thomas Jefferson, American Minister to France for five years from 1784, saw the Robert brothers go up for their third flight in a hydrogen-filled balloon. They set a record for time and distance, coming down over six hours later and 200 kilometres away, near Béthune.

Inside the gardens, take the path to the right to the **Musée de l'Orangerie**, the restored Classical pavilion which houses the finest small collection of art in this or any other city. There are 144 works from the Impressionists to 1930, a private collection left to the State by Domenica Walter on condition the paintings were kept together. The range includes landscapes by **Cézanne**, nudes by **Picasso**, **Monet's** *Argenteuil*, **Renoir's** series *Nus de Gabrielle* and **Sisley's** *Le Chemin de Montbuisson*. Presented on curved panels in its own salon are Monet's master works from his final years, eight murals of waterlilies *Les Nymphéas*.

Outside, walk to the **Octagonal Fountain** and continue down the central avenue past the manicured hedges and statues including eight bronze nudes by **Aristide Maillol**. One almost diving into the pond has a twin in the Museum of Modern Art in New York.

Pass the round pond, with children launching their model boats, towards the miniature **Arc de Triomphe du Carrousel**.

This was erected in 1808 to celebrate yet more of Napoleon's victories and part of the decorations were the famous four bronze horses taken from St Mark's in Venice. These were returned after 1815.

Walk back through the garden, turn right at Avenue du Général Lemonnier to Rue de Rivoli, with Terrasse des Feuillants to the left.

LUNCH: Cross to the other side of the Rue de Rivoli and turn left. On the corner with Rue d'Alger, the third junction, is the small pavement-café bar Rivoli Park. Service is fast and cheerful and the blackboard announces plats du jour such as a jarret de porc sur lit de choucroute - knuckle of pork with pickled cabbage; or choose one of the eleven salads.

Alternatively, turn into Rue d'Alger, then first left into Rue du Mont Thabor and at No 1 is the rustic l'Auberge de France. Choose either the restaurant with its exposed beams or the wine-cellar bistro below. The chef Zouad produces splendid specialities - canard à l'orange or saumon à l'unilatéral in the restaurant or a delicious pot-au-feu in the bistro. Children are made welcome.

Retrace the few steps to the corner of Rue de Rivoli and Rue d'Alger. The tour-bus office is to the left at No 214 and the double-decker coaches leave from the Tuileries side of the road.

The tour sets off by making a right turn towards the **Place Vendôme** where, on the right, among the elegant town houses, is No 12 where Chopin died at only thirty-nine years old. Next, round the flamboyant **Opéra** now mainly staging ballet and dance, to the department store district, including **Galeries Lafayette**. Past the main Gare St-Lazare railway station and back down by the **Madeleine** church to Place de la Concorde.

Through the traffic of **Place de la Concorde**, turning into the **Champs-Élysées**. Here the guide will enthusiastically point out the marks on the pavement where the guillotine was used - on King Louis XVI on 21 January 1793.

To the left after Le Nôtre's avenues of trees, are **Grand Palais** and **Petit Palais**. Beyond, on the left, is the entrance to the *Franklin D Roosevelt* station where building of the Paris métro began in 1900.

The **Arc de Triomphe** at the top of the avenue might well have been a gigantic elephant instead of an arch, if Napoleon had not changed his mind. The arch took thirty years to build and Napoleon did not live to see it finished.

Then along Avenue Kléber to the **Palais de Chaillot** with a perfect camera view of the Eiffel Tower. There are prestigious museums in each wing of the palais including Museum of the Cinema, which features the pioneering work of the Lumière brothers and Cinémathèque Française, one of the richest film libraries in the world.

The bus swings round over Pont d'Iéna and stops in Parc du Champ de Mars to view and photograph the **Eiffel Tower**. The city's celebrated landmark is 312 metres high, although now overtaken as the world's highest by the television tower in Tokyo. It takes 45,000 kilos of paint to redecorate.

The **École Militaire** nearby gives an opportunity for the guide to recall the academy's report on

Tuileries: model sailors

the 15-year-old Napoleon: 'Would make an excellent sailor. He is just an animal when seen on horseback.'

Past the **UNESCO** building with Henry Moore's *Figure in Repose* in the garden. Then on to **Hôtel des Invalides** where, below the French Classical dome gilded in bi-centenary year for the third time in its life, Napoleon is buried. The word *hôtel* in French describes a large private house and this was built by Louis XIV as a convalescent home for the war wounded.

Look to the right and catch a glimpse of **Rodin's** most famous sculpture *The Thinker* in the garden of the museum devoted to him.

Back towards the river, a right turn along Quai d'Orsay and across Pont de la Concorde to continue past the **Tuileries** and the **Louvre**. On the opposite bank is the old railway station now **Musée d'Orsay** with its feast of Impressionists. Further on the **Institut de France**, home of the **Académie Française** 'The Immortals'.

Past the town hall, **Hôtel de Ville,** through the narrow streets of the old area of **Le Marais** and into **Place de la Bastille**, now dominated by the new **Opéra de la Bastille**. The French Revolution started here in 1789 on 14 July - now a national holiday. **Colonne de Juillet** in the centre commemorates those killed in the riots of July 1830.

Across the Ile St-Louis, with the cathedral of **Notre-Dame de Paris** to the right, to the student quarter of the **Left Bank**.

Next landmark on the left is the **Panthéon**, where writers Victor Hugo, Voltaire and Émile Zola; inventor of the alphabet for the blind Louis Braille; and the symbol of the French Resistance in the last war Jean Moulin are buried.

Skirting the gardens of **Palais du Luxembourg**, which houses the Senate, upper house of the French Parliament, across Boulevard St-Germain, past the **Café des Deux Magots** and into the Rue Bonaparte, main centre for antique shops.

The bus returns along the side of the river to Rue de Rivoli.

TEA: At No 226 Rue de Rivoli is Angelina, one of the best tea-rooms in Paris. Try two of its delights: incomparable hot chocolate and Mont Blanc - meringue and chestnut purée.

Or walk just a little further along the Rue de Rivoli, turn right into the Rue Royale. On the right at No 16 is the world famous Ladurée, with the most exquisite macaroons.

11

This evening, return to Place de la Concorde to see illuminated some of the landmarks visited in daylight - from the Tuileries to the Assemblée Nationale.

DINNER: If the timing is right for the meal of a lifetime - with a bill to match - then the first evening in Paris is certainly the moment. At 41 Avenue Gabriel is Laurent (43 59 14 49). The setting is perfect - white and gold stucco Second Empire décor overlooking the Champs-Élysées gardens. Perfect too is Bernard Guilhaudin's cooking - oxtail pot au feu with cabbage or fillets of sole with fresh pasta are just two of his youthful accomplishments.

Or walk up the floodlit Champs-Élysées to Rond Point, turn right into Avenue Franklin D Roosevelt and right at the second junction Rue du Colisée. At No 34 is Le Boeuf sur le Toit, the most handsome of Jean-Paul Boucher's group of 1930s-style brasseries. Open until late, busy and friendly. ❏

Seeing the pyramids

**A view of the new Louvre and its works of art, a lunch of classic
Provençal cooking, walking Montmartre and the sparkle
of champagne and can-can at Moulin Rouge**

Once, Paris was the unrivalled world capital of art: painters flocked to live and work in the city. Since the post-war years, other cities such as New York and London have challenged that title.

Now Paris is fighting back. The enthusiasm for the arts shown by President Georges Pompidou and President François Mitterrand has released State money for new museums, improvements to existing ones and resources for acquisitions.

As a result, the number of visitors to museums has doubled. Also, many luminaries from the arts including painters, stage and film directors, writers, fashion designers and ballet dancers are being drawn to live and work in Paris. **The Louvre** is a visible sign of this

12

energetic new approach. At the entrance is the **Glass Pyramid**, designed by the Chinese-American architect Ieoh Ming Pei, a dramatic addition to the eight centuries of building, demolition, reconstruction and restoration. Deservedly, this monument of glass and metal, with its sides reflecting façades of the palace, has become the modern-day symbol of this national museum.

Inside, the presentation and layout of the works of art have been transformed, making the best use of the third more exhibition space. An early start is even more essential, so be at the doors before they open at nine o'clock and avoid the worst of the crowds. The nearest métro station is *Palais-Royal*, not the *Louvre* although its platforms are

Ⓜ Palais Royal

Musée du Louvre

well decorated with the museum's reproductions. *Palais-Royal* is so much easier and quicker - by the exit to Rue de Rivoli, through the archway leading to **Cour Napoleon** and into the pyramid to the entrance hall below.

From the information counter at the bottom of the escalator ask for a free leaflet, colour-coded for each floor and setting out room numbers. The eight multi-lingual receptionists who staff the desk are helpful and informative, part of the museum staff of one thousand. For more information, display screens detail special exhibitions, group conferences, film shows and changes to rooms or collections.

Worth buying from the book-shop to the left is a well-priced series of pocket guides *Petits Guides des Grandes Musées* (Editions de la Réunion des Musées Nationaux) with an edition for the Louvre and titles for other major museums including Versailles. The official catalogue for the Louvre, also available, covers every collection but is, understandably, expensive. Hall Napoleon includes rest rooms, telephones, a post office, *bureau de change* and shops selling reproductions, statuettes, coins and videos. Cassette players, with excellent guided tours in six languages, can be hired. There is also a room with nursery facilities.

Take the escalator to the mezzanine floor which overlooks the entrance hall. Study the scale model at the Richelieu entrance to appreciate the size and layout of the Louvre. The museum is on three levels, each colour-coded and U-shaped, with the area Richelieu on one side, Denon on the other, Sully at the end and the pyramid between the arms. These wings are divided into *arrondissements* each marked by numbers in square panels outside the rooms. This means that every work has an 'address', for instance the *Mona Lisa* - Denon 5 Purple or *Winged Victory of Samothrace* - Sully 7 Blue.

Set off for the entrance to the Denon section by going to the end 13

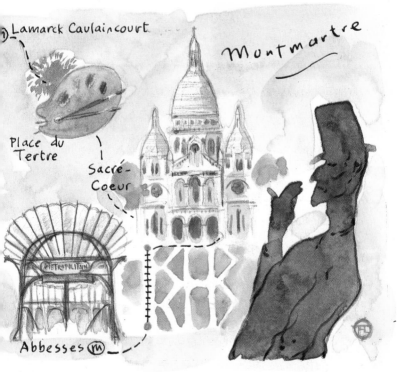

The Louvre pyramid: new identity

14

of the corridor, up the escalator and stop at the large room facing the pyramid. First gallery on the right leads to the Daru stairs in **Denon 3**. At the top is the dramatically-placed statue **Nike** or **The Winged Victory of Samothrace**, found on its Aegean island in 1863 and originally centrepiece of a fountain. The statue acts as a focal point for the whole museum and is a master-piece of the Hellenistic period.

Go to the left of the statue. In the first room on the right, after the rotunda, is **Galerie d'Apollon** built in 1661 to house the royal treasures, and the first interior decoration project **Le Brun** carried out for the royal family.

Enjoy the magnificent views of Paris from the window, then walk down to the end of the stateroom and, in the last showcase on the left, are the Crown Jewels. Among the most remarkable are the **Hortense** and **Regent** (137 carats) diamonds which once belonged to Cardinal Mazarin, a minister under Louis XIV and an art collector.

Return to *Winged Victory*, down a few steps and then up the stairs to the left. At the top on the left is **Denon 4**. Here are 17th century Dutch paintings, particularly the self-portraits by **Rembrandt** and

Bohémienne by **Frans Hals**. From the Dutch gallery go through to the long **Grande Galerie** which in the 17th century linked the King's Louvre Château to the Queen's Tuileries Palace.

The first large painting on the right is **Watteau's** *Embarkation for the Island of Cythera*. This painting of the crossing to the island of Aphrodite, the goddess of love, won instant fame when it was presented to the French Academy in 1717. The couples are walking down to the waiting boat and those on the right illustrate three stages of the same love affair. The painting is in complete contrast to Watteau's uncharacteristically large and light-hearted painting of a pierrot *Gilles* in his white suit.

Opposite, is a still-life *La Raie* by **Chardin** who was fascinated by themes of daily life. His career was launched by this stroke of brilliance. It was submitted to the Academy in 1728 and immediately earned his admission as a still-life painter, although, in those days still-life was considered the lowest category of art.

Carry on along the gallery until reaching the large sculpture of *Diana the Huntress*. Turn to the right, into **Denon 5**. On the left is the *Concert Champêtre* by **Titian**, previously attributed to Giorgione and the model for Manet's *Déjeuner sur l'Herbe*. Credit to Giorgione was understandable as the radiance of the figures and brightness of the scene are typical of the 'new style' introduced by the painters to Venice at the start of the 16th century.

At the far end of the gallery is **Veronese's** immense canvas *The Marriage at Cana* which he started and finished in 1562. Among the 132 characters at the banquet are, in the centre, Venetian painters masquerading as musicians - Titian in purple, then Tintoretto and, at the back, Veronese dressed in white as a cellist.

On the right-hand wall of this room in an hermetically-sealed chamber, surrounded by armoured glass is the **Mona Lisa**, more formally signposted as *La Joconde*. The fascination this picture has

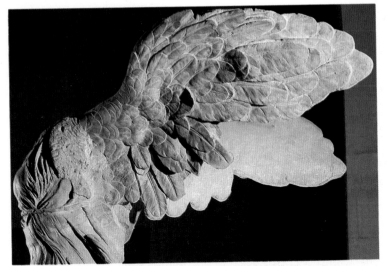

Dramatic: detail of 'Winged Victory of Samothrace'

Deserved credit: Titian's Concert Champêtre

held for hundreds of years is not just for her enigmatic smile but **Leonardo da Vinci's** subtle handling of light and shade. This technique of merging contours into the atmosphere, of softening edges in a diffused light is called *sfumato* which in Italian means 'misty' and gives the portrait its mysterious air.

Leonardo worked on the painting for four years from 1503.

The Louvre houses another 400 Leonardos, the biggest collection in the world, five of which are displayed alongside. These include his *Virgin and Child with Saint Anne* and *Virgin of the Rocks*, even greater in quality than *Mona Lisa*.

Leave the room by going to the left of the Veronese canvas for **Denon 2** with its view of the pyramid. Turn left into **Denon 1** and just inside the entrance, between two doors is the nude *La Grande Odalisque* by **Ingres**. The way Ingres stylized his models shocked the critics of his day. 'Beautiful forms are those that are firm, but full' he wrote. This harem slave justifies his words.

Walk back through **Denon 2** towards *Winged Victory*, seen in the distance, to **Denon 3**. This room contains large-scale canvases from 19th century France. The third picture on the left is **Théodore Géricault's** *Raft of the Medusa*. In 1816, the frigate *Medusa* was wrecked off the coast of Senegal and only fifteen of the 149 men on a life raft survived. Géricault, one of the founders of Romanticism, spent over a year interviewing survivors before painting this moving portrayal of desperation.

On the opposite wall, the last big painting but one is the *Death of Sardanapalus* by the brilliant colourist **Delacroix**. Inspired by Byron's *Sardanapalus*, it is an example of the expressive energy of Delacroix's Romantic style. The nudes are the most sensuous in French painting.

Continue past *Winged Victory*, down the stairs and on the ground floor turn towards **Sully**. At the end of the gallery, striking a model's

Seated Scribe: classic civil servant

pose, is **Venus de Milo**, described as 'our lady of beauty' and the most universally known work of art. This mutilated 2nd century BC statue of Aphrodite was found in 1820 on the island of Melos and symbolizes the Greeks' admiration for physical perfection.

Behind the statue, go down one flight of steps to the front of the large sphinx, then up the facing stairs towards Egyptian antiquities. At the top of the stairs turn right towards **Sully 6**. In the third room, in front of a glass case, is **The Seated Scribe**.

Carved in limestone in 2500 BC, it was discovered by Auguste Mariette in 1850. The figure, a civil servant, is sitting in the classic position of a scribe - legs crossed, a papyrus scroll across his knees and, once, a reed in his right hand for writing. One of the fascinations of this sculpture is the intense look in his eyes, an effect created by the use of quartz and crystal.

Go back to the first room **Sully 7** and on the right is one of the oldest examples of **hieroglyphic writing** on the tall limestone column found in the tomb of an early pharaoh, the Serpent-King.

Take the stairs back to the sphinx and turn right to walk round the medieval **dry moat**. Long before the Louvre was a museum or even a royal palace, there was a castle on this site, built in 1200 by Philippe-Auguste. At the end of the 17th century there was hardly a stone left standing of the original castle, even this moat was filled in with demolition rubble which stayed until as recently as 1984.

After the walk round the moat, leave for the second floor of Sully overlooking the Cour Carrée. Turn left towards **Sully 2** to **4**. In the second room is the *Avignon Pietà* the altarpiece by **Enguerrand Quarton**, a key figure in 15th century religious painting.

The portrait which faces the entrance of the next room is of *François I* by **Jean Clouet**. The emphasis by the Dutch artist is not on the sitter but the detail, in particular the crown motif in the weave of the purple brocade and the

16

17

The pyramid: see-through image of the new Louvre

Delacroix's 'Death of Sardanapalus': Romanticism and sensuous nudes

chain of the Order of St Michael round his neck.

After a short flight of steps, go right towards **Sully 3**. In the third room, on a large pillar in the centre, is a painting of three figures in torchlight *St Irene Mourning St Sebastian* by **Georges de la Tour**. He painted this in 1650, towards the end of his life, and the work reflects calm and silence.

In the next room, on the left-hand wall, is a set of four paintings of the seasons by **Nicolas Poussin** including his *Summer*, second on the left. The last room on this floor has four paintings of the life of *Alexander the Great* which, until the extensions to the Louvre, have never been on display. **Le Brun** began the paintings in 1661 and presented them in 1673, stopping midway because there was nowhere large enough to show them.

Return to the first room and, on the landing, take the right-hand stairs down to the mezzanine level.

18 **COFFEE: What better place to sit and digest the cultural excesses of the morning than the Café du Louvre off the main reception area below the new pyramid. Freshly-cooked filled croissants with coffee or tea, all cheerfully available.**

As the morning has been spent admiring art from the beginning of civilization to the 19th century it is time to step firmly into the present. Montmartre is the next destination. This artists' district still lives on, in the reflected glory of the generation of painters and writers who made it famous at the beginning of the century - van Gogh, Degas, Zola and Picasso.

Take the escalator to ground level and exit through the Pyramid and the arch of the Richelieu wing.

Cross to *Palais-Royal* métro. Destination station is *Lamarck-Caulaincourt* on line No 12. To get there from *Palais-Royal*, catch line No 1 in the direction of *Pont de Neuilly*. Get off at *Concorde* which is just two stops, and follow the signs *Correspondance Pte-de la Chapelle* which is the direction on line No 12. The station *Lamarck-Caulaincourt* is eight stops along.

On leaving the platform at *Lamarck-Caulaincourt* walk straight ahead to the lifts - ignore the steps on the right as it is a long climb to the exit. Outside, immediately left, up the steps to Rue Caulaincourt.

LUNCH: Finally reaching the top of the steps is a good moment to consider lunch. A short way down the Rue Caulaincourt on the right at No 57 is Le Clodenis, a much-praised Montmartre landmark specializing in Provençale dishes. Owner and chef Denys Gentes prides himself on his daily Menu Provençal. Typical three-course lunches include Mediterranean ratatouille or a soupe de poisson; fillet de merlan or lapin rôti au thym followed by a mouth-watering selection of desserts.

Outside, after lunch, turn left, walk to the junction and pick up the sign *Musée de Montmartre*. Cross the road and turn right into Rue des Saules which climbs to the top of the limestone **butte Montmartre**. Slow progress is made a pleasure by the country atmosphere and the views over Paris.

On the left, just before the crossroads and half hidden by an acacia, is the tiny **Au Lapin Agile**, the legendary cabaret of Old Montmartre. Immortalized by the pen and brush of the famous, from Picasso to Pissarro, it is still unspoilt - paintings against the walls and most evenings, the traditional literary debates as well as cabaret. As the evening goes on, the sing-along of French songs begins. The owner accurately describes his 'lively rabbit' as the only place to enjoy real funky French music.

Cross Rue St Vincent, past the last surviving vineyard in Paris with its plaque to the local folk hero Francisque Poulbot, the famous Montmartre illustrator of chubby little children who, in the thirties, battled to prevent developers taking over the land.

Take the next turn left into Rue

Sacré-Coeur: painters' muse

Cortot. On the left, in the house where Renoir and Utrillo rented studios, is **Musée de Montmartre**. Displays include old photographs, Toulouse-Lautrec posters and a re-creation of a 19th century bistro, complete with a well-worn zinc bar counter. From inside, there are delightful views of the vineyard and surrounding areas.

On leaving the exhibition, turn left along the cobbled street and then right. Walk straight ahead to be met by the first of many artists complete with sketch pads offering instant portraits. Slightly to the right is the picturesque but crowded **Place du Tertre**, usually overwhelmed as waiters from the open-air restaurants attempt to serve customers while artists fiercely demonstrate their unique style of assembly-line painting.

For a more tranquil view of Montmartre, leave by the left-hand corner of the square into the cobbled **Place du Calvaire** overlooking the steep steps with views of Paris in the distance. Keep bearing right and turn right into Rue Norvins; to the left is the crossroads so often featured by Utrillo.

Back past Place du Tertre and, on reaching the walls of St-Pierre Church, turn right. Follow the road round to emerge at the terrace overlooking the city beneath the white domes of **Sacré-Coeur**. Steps lead

to the porch and its three arches, above which are statues of two idols of French history, King Louis the Blessed and Joan of Arc. On top of the central dome is a belfry housing **La Savoyarde**, at 19,000 kilos one of the world's heaviest bells.

Inside the church, go to the north aisle and the entrance to the stairway leading to the dome gallery. From the top can be seen the mosaic-encrusted interior of the church and a panorama of Paris.

Outside the church, take the steps to the left and then bear right in front of the terrace and take the **cable railway** which descends into Place St-Pierre. Looking back there is a superb view of the towering Basilica of Sacré-Coeur.

Leave the square by the Rue Yvonne Le Tac for the return via the *Abbesses* métro station. Before going down to this deepest of Paris underground stations, pause to admire this **Hector Guimard entrance** with its original green glass roof, wrought-iron arches and amber tulip lights. There is only one other left in Paris, at *Porte Dauphine* near Bois de Boulogne. Examples of Guimard's work for the métro are in New York's Museum of Modern Art.

DINNER: The Moulin Rouge, brought to life by Toulouse-Lautrec in his poster paintings of the singers, clowns and dancers, symbolizes the night life of Montmartre. The first of two shows, at 10 o'clock, is the most popular. A booking through hotel or agent usually includes travel to and from the door and dinner.

Alternatively, make a direct reservation and choose between a table near the stage, with pre-show dancing and three-course adequate meal, or a seat further back for the price of a bottle of champagne or a minimum two drinks. The cabaret is firmly middle-of-the-road, the can-can dancing energetic but the audience of 850 tourists at each show reserves most of its applause for the speciality animal acts. ❏

19

Among the magasins

From tranquil Palais-Royal arcades to hectic department stores and the terrace of Café de la Paix to below ground at Les Halles and the rooftop at the Beaubourg

Shopping in Paris has always been an aristocratic business. Yet, while nurturing the assets of *haute cuisine* and *haute couture*, the city takes care to tempt the hesitant by making it as much a pleasure to browse as it is to buy.

This morning begins in the arcades where the young Louis XIV lived, moves to shops for the internationally wealthy and continues along the boulevards of the *grands magasins*, the cluster of world-famous department stores. Then, with feet more firmly on the ground, crowds are joined at the trendy, some would say outrageous Les Halles and the equally controversial Beaubourg Centre.

Start at the *Palais-Royal* métro and exit directly in front of **La Comédie Française**, the most prestigious theatre in Paris. Cross Place Colette, named after the mischievous writer of *Gigi*, and through the arches to the right of the theatre into **Jardin du Palais-Royal**. At the far end is the apartment in which Colette lived the last years of her life earlier this century.

At the end of the 18th century the king's cousin, Louis-Philippe d'Orléans, raised much-needed money by setting up arcades filled with boutiques round this royal quadrangle, modelled on the Piazza San Marco in Venice. His idea caught on and, until the Revolution, the sixty shops, cafés and gambling houses in the galleries named after his three sons Montpensier, Valois and Beaujolais had

20

attracted fashionable and wealthy Parisians. From offices in the apartments above, the Directorate of Fine Arts can admire its **Colonnes de Buren**. Completed in the mid-1980s, the 260 stubby black and white pillars of various sizes are dotted across the courtyard and protrude through metal grilles, below which are water canals and floodlights. It took a legal battle with shocked residents before the sculptures could be completed.

Today, the gallery boutiques with their tiny shopfronts are squeezed together in the arcades. They specialize in quaint curios such as second-hand medals and war decorations, puppets, musical boxes, antiques, rare stamps, coins, pipes, lead soldiers and from **Les Drapeaux de France** at 34 Galerie Montpensier, historical postcards - a change from tourist views.

Walk through the columns and take the left hand **Galerie Montpensier**. On the right are the gardens, surrounded by lime trees, where Camille Desmoulins called the people to arms on 13 July 1789 and which Marat described as 'the nucleus of the Revolution'. In the centre are fountains with sculptures by **Pol Bury**. Turn into **Galerie Beaujolais** at the far end and on the left is one of the most aristocratic restaurants in Paris - **Le Grand Véfour**. It was here that Victor Hugo hosted a party for the director and cast on the opening night of his controversial *Hernani*.

Return by **Galerie Valois,** known as the Prow gallery because of its nautical style. Richelieu, for whom the palace was originally built in 1632, was the Minister for the Navy. Back through the archway entrance, walk in front of Comédie Française. In the foyer is the chair in which the playright Molière was sitting when he was taken fatally ill. Around the corner is Visconti's **Molière Fountain** with his statue by **Seurre**.

On crossing to **Rue St-Honoré** there is a splendid view on the right of the façade of the Opéra. At first, Rue St-Honoré is narrow and still   21

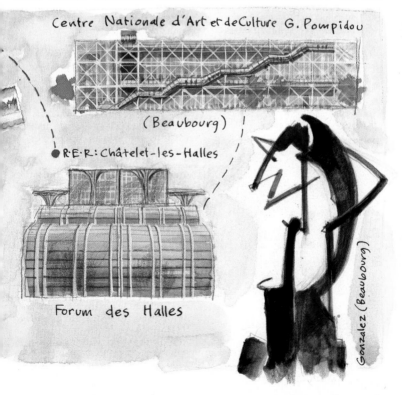

Centre Nationale d'Art et de Culture G. Pompidou

(Beaubourg)

R·E·R: Châtelet-les-Halles

Forum des Halles

Gonzalez (Beaubourg)

retains its character with small *boulangeries, charcuteries, épiceries* and *pâtisseries* among the lingerie and luggage.

COFFEE: The aroma of freshly-roasted coffee announces the arrival, just before the junction with the Rue des Pyramides, of Verlet at No 256. Among the open sacks of coffee beans and teas are a few seats to sample the contents, served in elegant cups accompanied by home-made pastries including its forte Tarte Apricot Verlet.

At No 233 is **E Goyard Aine**, founded in 1792 and one of the city's oldest shops, specializing in *articles de voyage;* but among the suitcases, some interesting small gifts. There is also everything, but everything, for the travelling pet poodle.

On the corner leading to Place Vendôme, the heady perfumes of **Guerlain** compete with those of its neighbour, the florist's shop. Here on the polished marble counters are displayed the range of perfumes, make-up and bath salts, many sold only in their five shops in Paris.

Turn right to admire **Place Vendôme**, the wealthiest square in Paris and one of the finest examples of 17th century architecture. In the centre is the 1806 victory column, 41 metres high, topped by a statue

Morabito: first catch a crocodile

of Napoleon as Caesar and cast in bronze from Austrian and Russian canons captured after the battle of Austerlitz.

Circling it are elegant town houses with arcades at ground level and, typical of Paris, dormer windows in the roofs. To the left is the **Ritz**, the most famous hotel in the world, which has counted Scott Fitzgerald, Gertrude Stein and Hemingway as regular guests.

Back to Rue St Honoré, across Rue de Castiglione, and on the opposite corner is **Morabito**, a rival to Hermes in leather goods, with cabin trunks, briefcases, handbags and shoe boxes. Its speciality for the *haut monde* is not leather but skins of alligators, ostriches, snakes and the rarest, crocodiles, with a two-month waiting list.

Next, alligators in a different guise - the **Lacoste** shop. Its symbol has been described as 'a $10 shirt with a $50 alligator' but, here in Paris, the chic is obvious, particularly in children's clothes.

Opposite is the **Hôtel France et Choiseul** where Franklin and Eleanor Roosevelt spent their honeymoon in 1905.

At the next junction is Rue Cambon where, a short way down on the left at No 14, is **Cadolle**. Inside this town house a century ago Herminie Cadolle, a Parisian seamstress, invented the brassière. The lingerie business now has an international client list, particularly royalty, and is run by her great-great-granddaughter Poupie.

Back in Rue St Honoré before the junction with Rue Richepance, is No 400 where Robespierre lived. It is now a restaurant called inevitably **Le Robespierre**. On the next corner is **Au Nain Bleu**, the most famous toyshop in the world. Inside, among the elaborate dolls' houses, matching furniture and toy trains, can be found puzzles at most prices - a speciality - and a herd of that irresistible elephant *Babar*.

Outside, from here to the Palais de l'Élysée the **Rue du Faubourg St-Honoré** demonstrates the art of window dressing with wit and style. And, almost to spoil it all, prices have to be shown by law - usually

22

Fauchon: perfect produce and gifts

very small and with one nought too many. Enjoy the windows to the full by continuing along the avenue beyond Rue Royale keeping to the right pavement, crossing the road before reaching the Palais de l'Élysée, with its resplendent Republican Guards, and returning along the other side.

The first showroom is another **Gucci** (four floors), then follows

Courrèges: charisma

Guy Laroche, **Yves St Laurent** (for men and women), **Courrèges**, and at Rue d'Aguesseau close to **St Michael's English Church** is the shopping mall **Sixty-two**.

Cross the road at this point and at No 41 is the residence of the **American Ambassador**. Next door is the **British Embassy** and further down is the **Japanese** equivalent, just three of the hundred elegant mansions among the shopfronts.

On this side are **Pierre Cardin**, **Lancôme**, **Gucci** (yet again) **Ted Lapidus** and **Cartier**.

On returning to the Rue Royale turn left towards **La Madeleine**, the 18th century church modelled on a Greek temple, known for lavish religious ceremonies and organ concerts. Society weddings and funerals for which it was famous have declined as the parish, once residential, is now the city's finance centre. Chopin's *Funeral March* was played here for the first time at his funeral and Josephine Baker was accorded a twenty-one gun salute at her service.

Circle round to the right past the restyled and expensive department store **Aux Trois Quartiers** to admire the flower market at the side of the church. The flowers on the stalls match the spectacular displays of fruit and vegetables in

23

the windows opposite at **Fauchon**, Europe's most luxurious food hall. The store boasts 20,000 lines, including a complete *charcuterie*. Presents to take home are more likely to be found across Rue de Sèze at the pâtisserie counter of the stand-up café or gift shop upstairs.

Outside, turn right into Rue Tronchet and, at the end, on Boulevard Haussmann is the 1865 department store **Au Printemps**, now much copied. The domed roof built by Brière in 1923 is now an historic monument. Collect a store leaflet in English to locate the departments. On the 4th floor of the new wing is *la rue de la mode* featuring avant-garde fashion names among the traditional labels.

Next door is the rival **Galeries Lafayette** built thirty years later and famous for its Art Nouveau staircase and dome of stained-glass and wrought ironwork finished with gold leaf. The big-name designers are on the *Tonic* and *Chic* floors as well as own-label clothes for which the family-owned store is rightly proud. From the top floor is an exciting view over the rooftops of the city.

LUNCH: Choose between the two Grands Magasins. The food hall on the sixth floor of Au Printemps serves anything from pizzas to grills though it hardly competes with the brilliance of the stained glass overhead. Next door at Galeries Lafayette follow the signs to the Galfa Club men's store and beyond is the elegant brasserie Le Pub with good waitress service or food at the bar. Start with a kir from a selection of five or a juice cocktail Le Jogging Drink with tomato, carrot and pear or Le Nice Complexion containing strawberry, orange, tomato and grapefruit. Stay with the chef's dishes of the day, particularly the fish, and for children Le Baby Pub steak, chips and ices.

On leaving the stores, cross over the Boulevard Haussmann and walk round to the main entrance of the grandiose **Opéra** - opulent and excessively ornate, almost an architectural parody. The designer was Charles Garnier, a young unknown chosen by a jury from an open competition which attracted 171 entries, including one from Viollet-le-Duc, much favoured by the Empress Eugénie. Garnier's work was finished in 1875 and a bust of him by **Carpeaux** is by the doors to the Loggia.

Because there was an under-

24

Galeries Lafayette: designer names under the dome

ground stream below the site, Garnier built a huge tank which acts as foundations for the theatre and still provides water for the city's fire brigade. This 'cellar' was the inspiration for Leroux's *Phantom of the Opera*, later a classic film and world-wide theatre musical.

Through the main doors is the magnificent white marble and onyx **Grand Staircase**. If rehearsals allow, follow this to the first floor and into the vast **Grand Foyer** with marble columns, balustrades and statues, surrounded by St-Gobain glass mirrors. The relatively small **Auditorium**, with five tiers of red and gold balconies and mysteriously deep boxes, is dominated by the 6,000 kilo chandelier adorned with gilt. In 1896, during a performance of *Faust*, it crashed down, killing a ballerina.

Above the chandelier, covering the original Lenepveu ceiling, is the circular canvas by **Marc Chagall**, a fantasy incorporating scenes from ballets like *Giselle* and operas such as *The Magic Flute*. He painted this as part of a twenty-year programme of renovation of the theatre. With the transfer of opera productions to the new Opéra Bastille, l'Opéra's ballet company of 152 dancers will now be able to take centre stage.

Cross to the Rue Auber and Boulevard des Capucines junction.

TEA: L'Opéra architect Garnier also designed the sumptuous green and gold rooms of Café de la Paix. Outside, under the distinctive umbrellas, the busy terraces have welcomed everyone from General de Gaulle to Dali. Enjoy a drink, a look at the passing crowds - and the stationary traffic.

When Baron Haussmann planned the boulevards of Paris, the Place de l'Opéra was the key junction, replacing the twisting maze of narrow streets.

A hundred years later, the city has completed an equally dramatic undertaking - the shopping and leisure complex of the **Forum des Halles**. This is the next destination.

Turn left, away from the

Les Halles: layers of shopping

square, along Rue Auber to the *Auber* métro and take the RER express line to *Châtelet-Les-Halles*, the largest underground station in the world.

Escalators emerge into four floors of cinemas, art galleries, restaurants and 180 stores and boutiques selling everything from records to designer clothes. For sport there is a glass-walled swimming pool and a gymnasium. Before this, Les Halles was a run-down area of the city described by Zola as *le ventre de Paris* 'the belly of Paris' and covered by Victor Baltard's abandoned iron and glass market halls.

The new Forum was the work of architects Claude Vasconi and Georges Penchréac'h. They created layers of glass and aluminium tunnels around a central patio **La Place Basse** and a pink marble sculpture of *Pygmalion* by the Argentinian **Julio Silva**.

Les Halles, with its 40,000 square metres of terraced selling space and outdoor cafés at each level, is a thriving commercial success. An example of this is FNAC, the group selling hi-tech electronic goods, which has its largest store on the second level. Each Saturday, 100,000 customers

Beaubourg: utilities on the outside

carry away cameras, videos, CDs, books and reduced-price concert tickets in its fashionable and distinctive carrier bags.

26 Follow the signs and pedestrian walkways to another extravagant and just as daring architectural achievement of the 1970s - the **Centre National d'Art et de Culture Georges Pompidou** or **Beaubourg** as it is more easily known. Since it opened in 1977, the centre has become the city's most visited attraction.

Cross Boulevard de Sébastopol and, on the other side of Rue St Martin, is this almost transparent 'art refinery' centre.

Pause to study the building from a distance. Particularly the way the architects, Englishman Richard Rogers and Italian Renzo Piano, have placed the utilities on the outside and coloured each one to match their original drawings.

Walkways are in red, electricity conduits in yellow, ventilation shafts are blue, water is coloured green and the structure is white. Escalators snake up a transparent tube woven into the tangle of pipes and tubes and take a constant stream of visitors to and from the five levels.

Before entering the centre, enjoy the entertainment offered on the sloping piazza - musical groups,

acrobats, mime artists, poets, orators supporting or opposing, even the band of the Salvation Army, all relying for support on spontaneous generosity.

Inside, ask at the *accueil*, the information desk, for a leaflet on events of the day. At the very least there are documentary audio-visual shows in the walk-in theatre in the **Grand Foyer** on the ground floor and, at the same level, an **Atelier des Enfants** - supervised children's events. Also on this floor is the **Industrial Design Centre**.

Step onto the escalator for the exhilarating ride to the top floor. This is an opportunity to locate the cultural attractions at each level. Reached from the second floor is the **Public Information Library**, mainly of the 20th century, with over one million books, videos and local and foreign newspapers, all available for free examination. Reference records are on three levels: literature, art, sport and leisure on the first, newspapers and magazines second and sciences and computers third.

The fifth floor contains the **Grande Galerie** where prestige exhibitions are held. These usually last several months.

Spreading out on the top three floors - the entrance is on the fourth - is the **National Museum of**

Au Pied de Cochon: nostalgia on the inside

Modern Art with Picasso, Gris, Chagall, Modigliani and Bonnard. At the terrace level are examples of Cubism and abstract art - *Grand Intérieur Rouge* and *La Blouse Roumaine* by **Matisse** and works by **Picasso**, including his *Femme Assise* of 1909. Later still is *Electric Chair* (1966) by **Warhol**.

As the escalator climbs, landmarks such as Montmartre, Eiffel Tower and Panthéon and the Tour St-Jacques with its solitary gargoyle can be seen. From the top floor looking back, is the Hôtel de Ville with its château-like chimneys.

APERITIF: On the top floor is the busy bar, terrace and self-service restaurant. The thin metal chairs and tables blend with the modernistic mood of the centre but the snacks are traditionally French.

Finally, as this is a shopping day with a difference, turn right outside the Beaubourg to the shopping mall **Quartier de l'Horloge** bounded by the Rue St-Martin, Rue du Grenier-St-Lazare and Rue Beaubourg. Stand in front of the huge electronic brass and steel clock. On the hour it springs to life. The clock is called *Le Défenseur de Temps*, Defender of Time, **Jacques Monestier's** sculpture weighing

1,000 kilos. Every hour the life-size warrior, armed with a double-edged sword, does battle with a bird, a crab or a dragon - symbolizing the elements. If the time is 6 pm, all three will attack - unsuccessfully.

DINNER: Return to Les Halles. One of the few streets left untouched to make room for the Forum is Rue Coquillière between Bourse de Commerce and the church of St-Eustache. At No 6 is Au Pied de Cochon, a landmark of the old Halles. There may be a wait but the restaurant is open twenty-four hours a day, a relic of Les Halles markets.

The nostalgic atmosphere is disturbed only by the bustling waiters balancing giant plates of fruits de mer. Order oysters to start or the name of the house, grilled pig's trotter with Béarnaise. Follow with roast rack of lamb - carré d'agneau rôti aux aromates; or fish - blanc de turbotin poché and Hollandaise; and finish with a chocolate gâteau and crème anglaise - gourmandise du curé de St-Eustache. After such an evening it is easy to understand why locals cling to memories of the district and resent intrusion of the new. ❏

27

Bridges and bayonets

**By boat along the Seine, by 260 steps to the top of Notre-Dame
and by foot through the Marais to Place des Vosges,
the city's oldest and prettiest square**

Paris was born on a river and still lives along a river. Having started life on two islands in the middle of the Seine - Ile de la Cité and Ile St-Louis - the city developed along its banks.

Today's tour begins on those islands. Take the métro to *Pont-Neuf*, cross the bridge and turn right into **Square du Vert Galant** - named after 'Gay Old Dog', Henri de Navarre, King Henri IV.

Moored alongside are *Bateaux Vedettes du Pont Neuf*, covered boats which leave every thirty minutes for an hour's trip, with commentary and refreshments on board. The tour covers the most interesting stretch of the river with which Paris carries on its love affair and provides an unusually angled and sheltered view of its landmarks. The boat moves off downstream under the **Pont-Neuf** itself. Ironically named, this is the oldest of today's thirty-five bridges across the Seine. Its twelve arches are decorated with the caricatures of members of Henri IV's court. Until 1813, a pump beneath one of them supplied the palaces of the Louvre and the Tuileries with water, of increasingly dubious purity. The fountain bore a plaque decorated with a statue of the woman of Samaria giving water to Jesus at the well, and is remembered in the name of the nearby department store, La Samaritaine.

The next bridge **Pont des Arts** is only for pedestrians. A 19th century first in France, it was built

28

of the latest material - cast iron. This was replaced by steel when the bridge was rebuilt ten years ago but every other detail, from the benches to the street lamps, has been faithfully reproduced.

To the right is a view of the Renaissance façade of the **Palais du Louvre.** Catherine de Médicis began building there in 1559 after her husband Henri II died in a jousting accident. Between **Pont du Carrousel** and the **Pont Royal**, the façade dates from around 1600 and the reign of Henri IV, first Bourbon king of France. It was rebuilt in the 19th century.

Immediately after passing under Pont Royal, on the left is **Musée d'Orsay**. Architect Victor Laloux, faced with the challenge of the Louvre across the river, veiled the cast-iron structure of what was to become a railway station with stone and stucco, combining practicality and elegance.

On the right is the **Jardin des Tuileries**, site of the palace in which Louis XVI and his queen were seized by revolutionaries in June 1792. Once under the **Pont de la Concorde**, the boat passes the **Assemblée Nationale**, France's Parliament building. Here, as on all government buildings, impeccably clean and bright tricolour flags are flown. One firm, Maison Festa, from its office near the famous tapestry factory of the Gobelins has the contract to ensure that the *bleu*, *blanc*, *rouge* flies over Paris pristine and untattered.

From the river, not much can be seen of **Place de la Concorde**, though the top of Mehemet Ali's **Obelisk** is visible. The river bends round, under the **Pont Alexandre III**. Erected for the Exhibition of 1900, its magnificent single span makes it the most picturesque of all the bridges.

Beyond the bridge, on the right bank are **Grand Palais** and **Petit Palais**, built using the same construction methods as for the Musée d'Orsay.

Under **Pont des Invalides** to **Pont de l'Alma**, named after the 29

Sailing past the landmarks

of Paris, kittens and weeping waifs, sit uneasily alongside the more sober books. Real bargains are rare but for the interested collector many of the stalls are a treasure house of specialist books.

Under **Pont St-Michel** and then **Petit Pont**, built where the Roman road from Orléans originally crossed a wooden bridge onto the island. Slowly past the **Cathedral of Notre-Dame de Paris** - a fine view of its flying buttresses from near the **Pont de la Tournelle**.

The boat rounds the peace and quiet of the Ile St-Louis and berths back at the Square du Vert Galant.

Walk along Quai de l'Horloge, past the Conciergerie, along Quai aux Fleurs and cross over Pont Saint-Louis. **Ile St-Louis** was originally two islets which were the setting for duels in the Middle Ages and, on one of which, cows were pastured. They were connected later. Ile St-Louis remains one of the quietest parts of the city with its *hôtels*, mansions of the 17th century, still intact.

Rue St-Louis en l'Ile with its fashionable boutiques runs the length of the island. In November, it is the setting for the procession of *Catherinettes*, in their fanciful hats. This began as a festival for all the workers in the millinery trade who were 25 years old and still unmarried - an Easter Bonnet parade but in weather less balmy.

COFFEE: Cafés can be found on every street; everyone who has visited Paris recommends the one they discovered. On one side of Rue St-Louis en l'Ile at No 24 is La Charlotte de l'Ile with a mouth-watering selection of pâtisseries and specializing in all manner of temptations in chocolate, and on the other at No 31 is Berthillon, with a well-deserved reputation for the sorbets and ices made here.

first Franco-British victory in the Crimean War, as are many London pubs. The bridge was undermined by the river and replaced in 1972. Only the figure of *Zouave* remains, a favourite landmark for Parisians and a high water mark. In the storms of 1910 the water reached up to his chin.

The boat turns round at the **Eiffel Tower**, with **Palais de Chaillot** on the opposite bank, to return to the islands. Fishermen line the banks, seemingly oblivious to the weather. Occasional catches of coarse fish are mostly returned. Joggers - hoping to avoid pollution from traffic - go *footing*, as it is called in France, along the lower quays. The Seine is still a trade route and there are barges from Switzerland, Germany and Holland, many bright with flowers on their decks, and with a moped or bicycle parked on the roof.

Under the Pont Neuf again, and alongside the **Quai des Grands Augustins**. Up on the wall can be seen the stalls of the *bouquinistes*. These little wooden 'hutches', often tightly closed and secured to the wall with chains, contain second-hand books. They are a symbol of a trade started in the 16th century although nowadays, coloured views

Back across the Pont St-Louis. Turn left and walk down to the tip of the island, the **Square de l'Ile de France**. Here is the **Mémorial de la Déportation**. A walk across the garden leads to steps and a

30

stark, rough-cast triangular court-yard, almost at water level.

In the floor of the underground sanctuary a flame burns on the **Tomb of the Unknown Deportee**. The words *Pardonne - n'oublie pas* 'Forgive - but do not forget' are a memorial to the 200,000 who did not return from Nazi labour camps.

Return to **Quai aux Fleurs** and on the front of Nos 9 and 11 are the sculpted heads of two famous 12th century lovers. This is where Abelard, tutor to the niece of Canon Fulbert courted and won the fair Héloïse, before the angry family had him castrated.

Turn left into Rue d'Arcole and into the **Place du Parvis Notre-Dame**, the spot from which all distances in France are measured. The name *Parvis* is a corruption of the old word for paradise, for it was in front of the cathedral, using the central doorway as 'Paradise', that early mystery plays were staged. These dramas brought to life gospel stories and works of the saints.

Enter **Notre-Dame**, standing back against the west door. Marvel at the huge nave, three tiers of Gothic arches soaring to a vaulted ceiling. Nine thousand people can stand here. Move forward to the transept to experience the full impact of the architecture. The **North Rose**, one of three stained glass windows, is visible still with much of its original 13th century stained glass.

Chapels between the buttresses surround the nave and among the many statues are a 14th century Virgin and Child, known as *Notre Dame de Paris* on the right pillar of the Chancel making a pair with *Saint Denis*, from the 18th century, on the left. Opposite is a simple tablet, unveiled in 1924, honouring the million from the British Empire who died in the first world war, the majority in France.

Outside, turn right along Rue du Cloître Notre-Dame and into the towers - home of Quasimodo, the Hunchback in Victor Hugo's novel. It was this book which first aroused public interest in the state of the Cathedral and led to its restoration. The entrance is at the foot of

Rose window: original glass

the **North Tower**. There are sixty steps, very steep, up to the gallery. Then another 200 steps to the platform between the two towers. Cross the bridge - home of the 'vampire' gargoyle who peers out across Paris, chin in hand. The view of flying buttresses, spire and the rest of Paris repays the effort.

The belfry, across in the **South Tower**, contains the great 13,000-kilo bell **Emmanuel**, tolled only on solemn occasions, and a museum tracing the history of the cathedral with the help of audio-visuals.

On leaving, cross the Place du Parvis, bear right along Rue de la Cité and into the **Place Louis Lépine flower market**. Flowers are replaced by caged birds on Sundays. Lépine was the Prefect who gave the Paris police their white truncheons and whistles.

Continue along Rue de Lutèce, cross the Boulevard du Palais and through the wrought-iron gates of the **Palais de Justice**, site of the 13th century palace and now the Law Courts. During the Revolution, the *tricoteuses* sat knitting in the courts as the \aristocrats were sentenced to the guillotine.

Follow the signs for **Sainte-Chapelle**. This wonder of Gothic architecture was built by Louis IX

31

in 1246 to house the Crown of Thorns and a fragment of the True Cross, purchased at exorbitant cost from Baudouin, the last French Emperor of Byzantium.

The many columns and arches of the **lower chapel**, originally intended for servants, supports the **upper chapel**. It was 19th century taste which decreed the excesses of alternate blues and reds, scattered with golden fleurs de lys.

Climb the spiral staircase, on the left, to the upper chapel. The lancet windows 15 metres high and separated by the slender pillars support the roof and give an overall impression of light and lightness.

Over 600 square metres of 13th century stained glass fill most of the wall space - an incredible achievement, even today, let alone 700 years ago. Even the faintest ray of sunlight illuminates the vivid colour and exquisite detail of over one thousand scenes from the Old and New Testaments.

Return to Boulevard du Palais, turn left and left again into **Quai de l'Horloge**. On the tower is the first public clock in Paris which gives the Quai its name, restored as it was in 1370.

Just before the twin towers take the entrance to the **Conciergerie**, the most famous prison in the world. The Seine used to flow right up to the foot of the four towers, the oldest of which, **Bonbec** - or babbler - earned its name from the loosening of tongues under torture. For two years from 1792 the jail was constantly filled with a thousand prisoners awaiting *le Tribunal*.

Enter the courtyard and on the right is the guardroom. Beyond, is the most impressive room on the ground floor the *Salle des Gens d'Armes*, Hall of the Men at Arms, hence *gendarme*. Go through the fine vaulted Gothic hall to the 14th century kitchens with walk-in ovens which once catered for 3,000 people at a time. Take the guided tour to explore the darker areas of the prison, including the women's yard, the prisoners' gallery and Marie-Antoinette's cell, part of which is a museum of The Terror displaying a blunt guillotine blade and other

gruesome reminders. Come out into the light of day, leaving dismal recollections of the past behind. Turn right along the river and cross Pont d'Arcole, the third bridge.

Ahead is **Hôtel de Ville**, the city's Town Hall. For 100 years until 1977, Paris was ruled directly by the government.

If there is an exhibition or meeting of the city council it is worth going inside to see the extravagant interior of Corinthian columns, elaborate staircase and Baccarat chandeliers.

The **Place de l'Hôtel de Ville**, in front, has been redesigned with fountains and without cars. This was once Place de Grève. As well as a site for executions it was a meeting place for the out of work. The expression *faire la grève* has subtly changed over the years; today it means to go on strike.

LUNCH: Continue along the Quai de l'Hôtel de Ville. On the left is Le Trumilou, run by Jean-Claude Dumont. From noon this homely bistro starts serving two fixed-price daily menus which are reliable and satisfying. The à la carte menu specialities from chef Alain Raymond include duck with prunes, canard aux pruneaux; calves' sweetbreads, ris de veau grand-mère; and an excellent

Sainte-Chapelle: wall of glass

32

roast lamb, gigot d'agneau. Or, walk on to the junction with **Rue du Pont Louis Philippe.** A sign announces the Marais, 'Quartier Historique' and here is the cheerful **Brasserie du Pont Louis Philippe.** Try the Greek salad with feta, followed by grilled daurade or moussaka and round off with either tarte citron or orange.

Climb the cobbled Rue des Barres behind the restaurant for a clear view of the Flamboyant Gothic buttresses of the church of **St-Gervais-St-Protais**. The façade was the first to be built in Classical style in Paris and combines Doric, Ionic and Corinthian architecture. The organ is the oldest in the city.

Continue up the narrow street - note the houses and the fine balcony at No 15 on the left - and turn right on reaching Rue François-Miron. On the right at No 68 is the dilapidated **Hôtel de Beauvais**. It was built for Anne of Austria's chambermaid Catherine Bellier as a reward for the sexual initiation of the sixteen-year-old Louis XIV. In its heyday in 1763 a seven-year-old Mozart was a guest at the hôtel and gave concerts for the royal family.

At the junction, cross the main Rue de Rivoli and into the Rue Pavée opposite.

REFRESHMENT: Too tempting to pass - at No 20 is the Pavé Glacé with perfect home-made ice creams.

Straight on, over the junctions with Rue du Roi de Sicile and the Rue des Rosiers. This last street is the centre of the Jewish quarter and, during the last world war, Nazis and the Vichy French marched down it to arrest and send thousands to concentration camps.

On the right-hand corner at the end of Rue Pavée, with an unusual square turret, is the **Hôtel Lamoignon**, the city's historical library and one of the largest and oldest houses in the Marais. Turn left into Rue des Francs-Bourgeois which is named after 'the men who

pay no tax' - the residents of 14th century almshouses.

On the left is a row of three beautiful houses. The first, **Hôtel d'Albret**, built in the 16th century was home of the widow of playwright Scarron. It was here she met Madame de Montespan then the King's mistress and was hired as governess at Versailles. Scarron's widow then took over as mistress, becoming Madame de Maintenon, later secretly marrying Louis XIV. Appropriately, it now houses the city's cultural affairs department.

Next door, walk into the courtyard to fully appreciate 17th century **Hôtel Barbes** and, finally, there is the **Hôtel de Coulanges** which was built in the 18th century. Cross to **Hôtel de Sandreville**, c1586 and continue along Rue Elzévir.

In the small Place de Thorigny at the end of the street is the magnificent and restored **Hôtel Libéral Bruand**, which houses the **Bricard Museum** or **Musée de la Serrure** specializing in the history of locks through the ages. The exhibits range from 20th century products of Bricard workshops to locks from Roman times and from the key to Marie-Antoinette's apartments to the symbolic gold key to the city.

Turn right into Rue de Thorigny and on the left is the renovated **Hôtel Salé** which now houses the outstanding **Picasso collection**, handed over to France to pay off inheritance tax following his death in 1973. The fact that the house itself was built in 1656 for a tax collector Aubert de Fontenay and paid for, and named, out of a levy on salt is coincidental.

On four floors is the largest collection of Picassos in the world - 230 paintings, 150 sculptures, 30 sketch books and 1,500 drawings as well as papers, photographs and his private collection of paintings and drawings by **Renoir**, **Cézanne**, **Rousseau**, **Braque** and **Matisse** donated by his widow Jacqueline.

Climb the wide staircase with its intricate wrought ironwork, a smaller version of the one at l'Opéra. On the third floor there are films on Picasso's life and work.

33

The second floor holds part of the private collection. Then, on the first floor, start with *Self Portrait* from his Blue Period and continue with Pink and Cubist influences and Surrealism, briefly in the 1920s. His sculptures, paintings and drawings from the 1930s are on the ground floor and those from the war years, 1950s and 1960s, including ceramics, are in the basement.

TEA: Just above the bookshop in the basement is a small restaurant serving fresh tea and a good selection of fruit tarts.

Turn back into Place de Thorigny, leave through Rue du Parc Royal and take the second right Rue de Sévigné. This street is named after the lady who spent the last nineteen years of her life at **Hôtel Carnavalet**, No 23 on the right. It was from here in the 17th century that she wrote letters to her daughter full of gossip describing the day-to-day happenings at the royal court and in the city. This collection of letters is now famous in French literature. Since 1889 this Renaissance mansion has been the city's Museum of History. It now extends next door to **Hôtel le Peletier de Saint-Fargeau.**

In the courtyard is a statue of

Louis XIV by **Coysevox**, one of the few royal bronzes to escape being melted down in the Revolution. On the keystone of the arch is the sculpture *Plenty* by **Jean Goujon**, who also carved the nearby lions.

On the ground floor are the **Salon d'Uzès** and **Café Militaire** both decorated by Ledoux and above is the **Henriette Bouvier Collection** - a group of rooms filled with beautiful pieces of Louis XV and XVI furniture, also a large **Brunetti fresco**.

Go through to Le Peletier, where on show is a model of the guillotine and memorabilia of the revolutionary years: the young Dauphin's exercise book; a rope ladder used for an escape from the Bastille; and the last letter from Robespierre, stained with his blood. Also the **Fouquet jeweller's shop** at the turn of the century decorated by Mucha, the rooms of writers Proust, Anna de Noailles and Paul Léautaud and the **ballroom of Madame de Wendel** painted by José Maria Sert in 1923.

Before leaving, enjoy the secluded courtyard gardens.

Outside, take the Rue des Francs-Bourgeois to the left, which crosses Rue de Turenne and leads to **Place des Vosges**, the oldest square in Paris.

In the centre are gardens, trees and three fountains, all illuminated at night. Overlooking the square are thirty-six matching houses with red and gold brick and stone façades, dormer windows, steep slate roofs and tall chimneys. Work on the buildings, all historic monuments, has been going on for the past two decades.

Start by walking down the right-hand arcade and **No 17** is where writer and orator Jacques-Benigne Bossuet lived. **No 13** has returned to its former glory as one of the square's most elegant buildings and the second floor of **No 9** is the meeting place for the Architecture Society which has restored the façade and shutters.

Follow the arcades to the left and try the door to the courtyard at **No 3**, beautifully painted with an attractive small garden. By the

34

Picasso: portrait of Dora Maar

Place des Vosges: 'Les Miserables' among the monuments

archway entrance, with a stone balcony and a bust of Henri IV, is **No 1** where Madame de Sévigné was born.

Past **Pavillon du Roi**, where odd numbers end and even numbers begin, in the corner at **No 6** Victor Hugo wrote *Les Misérables*. There is a small museum devoted to him on the top three floors which he once rented.

At the end of this side of the square turn right out of Place des Vosges into Rue du Pas de la Mule. At No 6 is the **Boucherie** with metal hooks above the door to hang meat. The butcher's shop has been in the Bissonet family for several generations but the present owner is more enthusiastic about musical instruments and has chosen to fill the shop with every sound imaginable. There is a tuba made of Venetian glass, violins and trumpets - even a piano built for a roundabout which also reproduces the sound of twenty-nine flutes, mandolins and violins.

Continue along and turn right to the Place de la Bastille with the symbol of liberty, *Génie de la Bastille*, sculpted by **Dumont** in the centre. Opposite is the **Opéra Bastille** opened as part of the city's bi-centennial celebrations. It was designed by Canadian Carlos Ott who was selected from 750 entrants in an international architectural competition. His auditorium can hold 2,700, triple the size of the audience at Garnier's Opéra.

This increase in seating means a strengthening in the quality of production, reduced cost of tickets and encouragement for the young to appreciate opera - a reminder after a day enjoying the city's past that its future looks likely to be just as dramatic and exciting.

35

DINNER: Today ends near to where Paris began on l'Ile St-Louis. Take the métro to Pont Marie. Cross the bridge and turn right into Rue St-Louis en l'Ile where at No 41 is La Taverne du Sergent Recruteur. Its name harks back to the days of naval press gangs when Recruiting Sergeants ensured enough food and especially drink was on offer to likely recruits. Leaded windows, heavy benches and tables on a stone floor add to the atmosphere. Arrive with a good appetite. The fixed price menu is lavish and includes ample wine. The speciality of the house is the first course which is sausages of all sorts, sizes and piquancy. And served with a knife sharper than the old Recruiting Sergeant's bayonet. ❏

A glorious renaissance

Ascend a refreshed Eiffel Tower, walk among Rodin's masterpieces, taste Basque food and from behind a station clock admire Renoir, Manet and Degas

It was the turn of the century and Paris was enjoying its *Belle Époque*. Horse-drawn buses and *fiacres* were crowded with Parisians admiring their new boulevards, the Opéra and racing at Longchamp. In Montmartre, the can-can dancers of the Moulin Rouge and the Lapin Agile were drawing packed houses.

The new Métropolitain railway was the pride of the city, together with electric light, which had its own pavilion at the Great Exhibition of 1900. Paris was a brilliant star in Europe's firmament - the paintings and sculptures of Degas, Renoir, Rodin, Manet, van Gogh, Cézanne and Toulouse-Lautrec all admired.

La Belle Époque died on the battlefields to which the taxis of Paris took the troops in 1914. Those who returned would never recapture the graciousness and the sparkle - France and the world had changed. Today revives Paris' *fin de siècle* atmosphere in the landmarks and works of artists who left their experiences, homes and lives in sculpture and paint.

First take the métro to *Place du Trocadéro*. In the centre of the square is the **equestrian statue of Marshal Foch**, commander-in-chief of Allied armies in the first world war.

On the far side is the smaller Yorktown Square with a **statue of Benjamin Franklin** who lived nearby and introduced to France his invention, the lightning conductor.

Walk through to the terrace of **Palais de Chaillot**, re-styled in

36

1937 for the International Exhibition of Arts and Techniques, to admire the view and the fountains and water jets of the formal gardens which stretch down to the river.

The two wings on either side are now four museums: to the right, the Maritime museum and Musée de l'Homme; and to the left, the museums of French Monuments and the Cinema.

Walk down the sloping gardens towards the Seine and cross the Pont d'Iéna. After the defeat of Napoleon at Waterloo, Marshal Blücher said that this bridge should be blown up as it was named after a Prussian defeat. Louis XVIII said that he would sit in the middle of the bridge if that happened. The bridge and the name stayed.

From here the massiveness and audacity of Gustave Eiffel's **Eiffel Tower** can be appreciated. Built between 1887 and 1889 from steel and cast iron, materials of the new industrial age, 300 acrobatic workmen assembled seven million kilos of girders, using two and a half million rivets. Its height is 312 metres with a television mast extending another eight metres. Astonishingly, its bulk exerts no more pressure per square inch than the four legs of a chair with a man sitting on it.

It is repainted every seven years and to begin its second century Eiffel's flagpole has been reinforced, renovated and cleaned.

Buy a ticket for the two-stage journey to the top - do not be put off by the waiting lines, the queues move steadily. To be able to claim to have reached *le sommet* of the Eiffel Tower makes it well worthwhile. Enter the upper storey of the two-deck lift, exit at the second floor (130 metres) and wait for a lift to the top (274 metres).

Through the glass walls of the electronic lifts from the second floor can be seen the interlaced criss-cross girders and the 292 floodlights which illuminate the structure at night. At the top of the tower, windows in the glass-enclosed platform look out on the

37

Palais Bourbon

Musée Rodin

Musée d'Orsay

Eiffel Tower: all the way to le sommet

city landmarks, clearly signposted. Through an interior window can be seen the office that Eiffel used and even, in wax, Gustave Eiffel himself and an 1889 visitor, Thomas Edison.

Return to the second level with its shops and souvenirs and then, by lift, to the first floor.

COFFEE: After the excitement of le sommet and the lifts, relax with coffee and croissants in La Belle France located in the new pavilion. This is an opportunity to write home, using cards with special postage covers from the tower's post office alongside.

Before returning to ground level, look in on the small cinema on this first floor to see an excerpt from the video history of the tower. After that, as an appropriate finish, take the ten-minute walk down the final flight of steps. Walk through the gardens of **Champ de Mars** where, on gravel patches under the trees, players of *pétanque* hurl *boules* or gossip.

The **École Militaire** now houses French officers studying advanced war training. It was here that a fifteen-year-old Corsican was admitted in 1784. He passed out with the report: 'Will go far if circumstances are favourable'. His name was Napoleon Bonaparte.

Turn right on reaching Avenue de la Motte, cross Avenue de Suffren and immediately on the right is **Village Suisse**, a gathering of antique shops and second-hand dealers selling mostly furniture. Not quite Belle Époque but almost.

Return to Avenue de Suffren, turn right and then left into Avenue de Lowendal which runs between École Militaire and the uninspired UNESCO building. Walk past the **Dome Church** of the **Invalides** where, in the rather dreary crypt, is the body of Napoleon. His son died in Vienna in 1832 and on 15 December 1940, exactly 100 years after Napoleon's funeral, Hitler ordered the return of L'Aiglon's ashes to lie beside his father. Paris, cold and hungry under the Nazi occupation, was not over-impressed: 'It is not ashes we need, it is coal'.

Turn left at Boulevard des Invalides and after 300 metres turn into the Rue de Varenne and the entrance to the magnificent **Hôtel Biron**. From 1908 until his death in 1917 this was the home and studio of Auguste Rodin, the greatest French sculptor of modern times. Rodin left his collection to the State and it is displayed in the gardens and the house to form the **Musée Rodin**.

Collect the free plan at the entrance showing the location of each work. Within the museum are 7,000 of his drawings, sketches and sculptures, including his most sensitive works *The Kiss*, *The Cathedral* and *The Man with the Broken Nose*. There are also works by **Renoir**, **Monet** and **van Gogh**, including the famous *Père Tanguy*. In the vestibule is Rodin's powerful *Walking Man* and in the first room,

Rodin: famous 'Thinker'

in complete contrast, the delicate *Girl in a Flowered Hat* and the bust *Mignon*. This is very probably of Rose Beuret, who bore Rodin a son in 1866 and whom he married in January 1917, two weeks before she died. Rodin died that same year.

Among the large-scale bronzes in the trees is the statue group *The Burghers of Calais* - one of ten versions to be found in museums around the world, all cast from the model kept here. Preparatory studies, which fill room 11 of the museum, give further insight into Rodin's work on this group.

Opposite, in the garden, is his most famous sculpture *The Thinker* and against the garden wall *The Gates of Hell*, commissioned by the State in 1880 as the gate to the Musée des Arts Décoratifs and on which he worked until his death, not living to see it cast in bronze.

In the middle of the pond is the sculpture *Ugolino*. Also in the garden are the *Victor Hugo* and, right of the house, his robed *Balzac*.

On leaving, return to the Boulevard des Invalides, turn right towards the Seine and along Rue de Constantine. This is the area of diplomatic and government offices. Before Quai d'Orsay, a plaque on the wall to the right marks the deaths of a French tank crew in

39

1944. There are many similar monuments in the city, often marked by a posy of flowers - an anniversary still remembered.

Walk along the Quai d'Orsay and, by the side of the closed gate of the ministry of Foreign Affairs, is the monument to French statesman **Aristide Briand**.

His words carved on it strike home: *Men have appointed judges to avoid unnecessary strife over small matters. Nations would do well to do the same to avoid drenching battlefields in blood. Each time a country avoids a war, that country has won a victory.*

Next, behind the gardens over-hanging the quai is Hôtel de Lassay, residence of the president of the **Assemblée Nationale** which is next door in **Palais Bourbon**.

Continue along Quai Anatole France past Hôtel de Salm, home of the **Légion d'Honneur**. The hôtel was built in 1786 by Pierre Rousseau for a German prince, Frederic III of Salm-Kyrbourg. The Legion was founded by Napoleon to reward public service. Displayed in the museum are orders and decorations illustrating its history.

LUNCH: Turn right into Rue de Bellechasse, left at Rue de Lille, right for Rue de Poitiers

Renoir: the mood of 'Le Bal du Moulin de la Galette'

40

and into the narrow Rue de Verneuil, where at No 51 on the right is Auberge Basque. Johnny and Bernadette serve typical dishes from the Basque provinces of south west France. A haunt of rugby players - for the south west provides many members of the French national XV - and discerning editors from nearby publishing houses.

After lunch, retrace steps to Rue de Bellechasse and into the entrance of **Musée d'Orsay**. When the Gare d'Orsay railway station and hotel were built for the 1900 World Fair, it was said 'the railway station

looks like a Palais des Beaux-Arts, and the Palais des Beaux-Arts looks like a railway station, so let us switch their functions while there is still time.' It took until 1986 for at least part of the idea to catch on.

The displays, in uncluttered galleries, cover art from the period 1848 to around 1914 and bridge the artistic gap between the Louvre and the Beaubourg. Coats, bags and umbrellas have to be left at the entrance. Pick up here the free English-language *Brief Guide* which indicates the A-Z sequence of rooms to view and paintings and sculptures to see.

Leather couches and chairs are provided for relaxed viewing and cameras can be used everywhere except the temporary exhibitions. As well as the leaflet, there are explanatory pages in plastic mounts available from wall racks.

A reproduction of the **François Rude** sculpture *La Marseillaise, Departure of the Volunteers*, from the Arc de Triomphe is mounted on the wall of the **entrance hall** and **Carpeaux's** *La Danse* which caused a furore amongst puritanical critics when unveiled in 1869 stands near the end of the main hall. This is part of a display devoted to l'Opéra which includes backstage machinery and, beneath thick glass in the floor, a model of the Opéra.

Also on the **ground floor** are early works of **Renoir**, **Monet** and **Manet**, particularly his *Déjeuner sur l'Herbe* and *Olympia*.

Move from here to the **upper level** with the advantage of natural light and move in time from Impressionism to the beginning of Modern art. Here are later **Renoir** outdoor scenes, the familiar *Bal du Moulin de la Galette;* **van Gogh's** *Self Portrait;* and a collection of **Cézanne**, particularly his still-life *Pommes et Oranges.*

L'absinthe is here, about which a lady angrily asked **Degas**: 'Why are all the women in your paintings so ugly?' He replied: 'Because, madame, most women *are* ugly!'

Among the neo-Impressionists is a fascinating collection of delicate pastels by **Toulouse-Lautrec** of the Montmartre nightlife including

41

La Danse au Moulin Rouge. Because of their fragility they are shown in a gallery away from the light of the main windows.

REFRESHMENT: Fascinating on this floor is the view looking through the giant station clock. Further along there is a twin clock in the Rooftop Café. Watch the minutes tick away with a drink or a pastry.

Walk down to the **middle level** where the displays, in time sequence, precede those in the Beaubourg. Three rooms facing the Seine are devoted to Art Nouveau: works by **Gallé** and others of the Nancy School; **Dampt**, **Carabin**, **Charpentier**; and **Hector Guimard** of métro fame.

On the terraces are the sculptures of **Rodin** and on the far side are the works of 20th century painters including **Klimt**, **Matisse** and the Fauvists - the short-lived Modern art movement at the turn of the century. Naturalism is shown in canvases such as **Cormon's** *Cain*, **Lionel Walden's** *Cardiff Docks* and the sculpture *Blacksmith*

by **Meunier**. Among the Symbolist paintings of **Burne-Jones** and **De Chavanne** is **Winslow Homer's** *Summer Night*, an evocative image of the mystery of the ocean.

Before leaving the museum and its 2,500 paintings and pastels, 1,500 sculptures and 1,300 photographs, pause to study both the **interior and riverside frontage**. As a railway station, its heyday lasted for forty years.

It was the departure point for 200 long-distance trains a day linked to sixteen underground lines. Electrification and its too-short platforms relegated it first to a suburban station and then, by the sixties, it was abandoned.

Its *Belle Époque* grandeur still created a suitable setting for General de Gaulle to announce his coup d'état in 1958; Orson Welles to film *The Trial* by Kafka in the great hall; and Bertolucci to use it for *The Conformist*.

Only public outrage forced the government to list the building as a protected monument and save it from developers. It took eight years in the eighties for the conversion work to be completed. **Victor**

42

d'Orsay masters: Manet's 'Déjeuner sur l'Herbe'

Musée d'Orsay: time recaptured

Laloux, who designed it at the turn of the century would certainly have approved the change.

TEA: Leave Musée d'Orsay by its elegant bookshop into Quai Anatole France, turn right and take the first right, Rue du Bac. No 46 is where chef-owner Christian Constant dispenses his lemon meringue tarts and brioches with a selection of nineteen varieties of tea. Two essential take-aways are his speciality chocolate bars and biscuits.

This evening, for dinner return to where this Belle Époque day started - the Eiffel Tower.

DINNER: Le Jules Verne restaurant on the second floor of the Eiffel Tower has achieved recognition not just for its views and grey and black décor by Slavik. Chef Louis Grondard's classical-based specialities are turbot with clam sauce and sweetbreads with mushrooms in pastry. Bookings (45 55 61 44) are essential if only to use the private lift.

Or, for a more typical (although fashionable) French bistro try Chez Maître Albert at 8 Rue de l'Abbé Groult but be sure to book (48 28 36 98) before setting out. Paintings provide an appropriate back-cloth for the artistry of chef Michel Civel. Try his speciality bouillabaisse en filets.   ❑

43

... and Cézanne's still-life 'Pommes et Oranges'

Palace of privilege

Visiting the home of the Sun King, from the Gilded Salon to the Hall of Mirrors, then into the gardens and later a romantic dinner on the Seine

It may seem an extravagance to devote a whole day out of seven to a one-time hunting lodge thirty minutes away from the city but to visit Paris and not see the **Palace of Versailles** would be sad.

The palace is France's proud symbol of monarchy, surviving even the Revolution. During the first world war, Versailles was the headquarters for the Allied War Council - the 1919 peace treaty was signed in the Hall of Mirrors. In 1944 it was taken over by Allied Supreme Command until the war in Europe ended. More recently, the palace welcomed Queen Elizabeth II and ex-President Reagan to France.

Though building of Versailles was begun in a small village as a hunting lodge by Louis XIII it will always be connected with his son Louis XIV, the Sun King, who came to the throne as a boy of five and ruled from 1643 to 1715.

Louis had a taste for splendour, for extravagance. He employed the landscape designer Le Nôtre, architects Le Vau and Hardouin-Mansart and interior designer Le Brun to build a palace which would outshine the magnificent château of his Finance Minister, Fouquet, at Vaux-le-Vicomte.

Twenty thousand workmen and six thousand horses raised the hill on which the château stands and transplanted whole forests to lay out the gardens. Alterations went on until 1710 when the 72-year-old Louis was finally satisfied.

Leave Paris - avoid Mondays

44

when the château is closed - by the commuter train (Line C) which runs along the Left Bank of the Seine to Versailles *Rive-Gauche* station.

From east to west, within Paris, there is a choice of stations - *Gare d'Austerlitz; St-Michel*, opposite Notre-Dame; *Quai d'Orsay*, by the Musée d'Orsay and the Légion d'Honneur; the *Invalides; Pont de l'Alma*, on the Left Bank, not the métro station; *Champ-de-Mars*, close by the Eiffel Tower; and *Javel*.

On coming out of the *Rive-Gauche* station, turn right and first left. In a few metres the wrought-iron black and gold grille of the gates leading to the **Ministers' Courtyard** can be seen in front of the palace. On either side of the avenue are the **stable blocks**, relics of the heyday of Versailles.

Louis XIV sold off land in what became the town of Versailles for five *sous* per acre, as long as the houses built were in line with the town plan and did not interrupt the royal view. Roofs were not allowed to rise higher than the level of the

Marble Courtyard in front of the central part of the palace. Court etiquette in those days demanded that 3,000 ministers and servants of the king were always in attendance. Court life was 'public' with the king and queen performing ceremonies of rising in the morning, eating and retiring at night - all under the gaze of their subjects.

Any citizen was admitted to the palace 'provided he was decently dressed'. Petitioners sought to catch the king's attention and it was believed, as in many courts of Europe, that the sovereign's touch could cure certain ailments.

At the entrance to Ministers' Courtyard, turn and look back over the town and the converging roads. The Romans may have thought that 'all roads lead to Rome' but in the France of Louis XIV all roads led to the Palace of Versailles.

Walk up to the **equestrian statue** of the king by Cartellier, placed here by Louis-Philippe in 1837, whose efforts and personal fortune helped save the château as 45

a national monument and museum. It was at this time that the inscriptions were placed on the façades of the two wings of the **Royal Courtyard** - *À toutes les Gloires de la France*. After the first world war, American millionaire John D Rockefeller paid for more restorations and a plaque to him is in the main hall. Take **Entrance 3** to the left for a guided tour of the King's Apartments and the Opera followed by a non-guided tour of the State Apartments, Hall of Mirrors and Queen's Apartments.

The visit begins in the **Guard Room**. It was here that any subject had the right to petition Louis XIV. Then comes the **Ante-Chamber**. Restoration of gilded wood carvings around the doors and windows is still in progress. The necessary

The ornamental pond designed by Le Nôtre: opulence among oppression

skills are rare today, the process requires the application of fine gold leaf sheets on a special glue and then laborious burnishing.

The second ante chamber is the **Ox-Eye Salon**, named after the round window high on the wall. This was where courtiers awaited the *Lever* and *Coucher* - the king's ceremonial rising and going to bed.

The **King's Bedchamber** at the heart of the château and with windows facing onto the Marble Courtyard, was the scene of these rituals. Louis XIV died here in 1715. Brocade wall coverings and gold-embroidered bed curtains were woven in Lyon to 1730 designs - a glimpse of the dazzling splendour of the court of the Sun King.

Next is the **Council Chamber** where in 1775 the decision was

taken to help the American colonies in their war of independence against the England of George III. At this time France was a great power in Europe - a population of twenty-five million compared to ten million in Britain and five million in America. Her help was crucial. The gilding has been sumptuously restored and the blue and gold drapes re-woven in Lyon, home of the silk industry.

The **King's Bedroom**, where Louis XV died from smallpox in 1774, and the next four rooms, which make up the **King's Private Apartments**, are much as they were during his reign.

Next to the suite is the **Clock Drawing Room**, named after the astronomical clock it contains. The movement was designed by Passemant, made by Dauthiau and placed in a gilded bronze case by Caffiéri. Movements of planets around the sun, phases of the moon, day and date are all recorded, as well as the time until 31 December 9999. The family would gather each New Year's Eve to watch the clock register the change of the year.

Nearby, a stairway allowed the king to reach the private apartments on the second floor, without having to pass through the Bedchamber and Council Chamber. This stairway is close to the **Ante-chamber of the Dogs** and the **Hunt Dining Room.** The names speak for themselves. The king hunted in the vast estates around Versailles on at least three days a week and in the evenings the dogs had a room to themselves while the king and companions dined next door.

Next door in the **King's Private Study** is the massive, 1,000 kilo, roll-top writing desk in which Louis XV kept his private papers. The gilded bronze frame supports an inlaid marquetry-work desk, to which only the king had a key. Tucked away at the left-hand side, however, just above the inlaid porcelain panel of *The Three Graces*, is a secret drawer into which, every day, his secretary would place ink, papers and quills which the king needed. On the coins and medals chest is a candelabra presented by a grateful, young United States

depicting the Gallic cockerel triumphant over the chained and cowering leopards of England.

Madame Adélaïde's Gilded Salon was created by Louis XV for his favourite daughter and it was here that a seven-year-old Mozart played for the family. The white and gilded walls made it a perfect setting for the king's coffee parlour in which to display part of his gold dinner service. Coffee was grown in the hot-houses of the Trianon so that guests could enjoy the king's fresh-roasted coffee.

The **Louis XVI Library** was designed by Gabriel for the young king on his accession in 1774 and is one of the finest examples of Louis-XVI-style decoration. Close by is the **Games Room** with its mirrors, fireplace, gilded walls and matching brocade on chairs and curtains - a replica of the original room.

Continue to the **Royal Opera** built by Gabriel for the marriage of Louis XVI in the short time of twenty-one months. Because the ground was not particularly solid, Gabriel built this 700-seater opera house completely of wood, which gives it fine acoustics. Inside, the wood is painted to look like blue and rose marble. A ceiling canvas depicts Apollo crowning the artists.

Originally, machinery below the auditorium raised the stalls to the level of the stage, turning it into a ballroom for 1,500. The curtain has to be raised upright because the coat of arms embroidered on it contains over nine kilos of gold and cannot be rolled.

The guided tour finishes here and to reach the more public apartments walk through the north wing to the chapel.

The chapel, the last of its kind to be built inside a palace in France, is dedicated to Louis IX, builder of the Sainte Chapelle in Paris. The organ is situated over the altar because the traditional place for it - over the west door - is taken up by the **King's Gallery** with its carpet woven at the Gobelins in 1760.

Hercules Salon is named after the **François Lemoyne** painting on the ceiling. It was originally built and decorated as a fitting setting for

Queen's Bedchamber: prolific succession

Veronese's *Christ in the House of Simon the Pharisee*, given to Louis XIV by Venice.

First of the suite of **Grand Apartments**, six reception rooms named after paintings decorating the ceilings, is the **Salon of Abundance** with its black and gilt boulle 17th century buffets, which held the drinks - hot chocolate, fruit juices and liqueurs - for the weekly court receptions.

In the **Venus Salon**, with its marble décor still intact, courtiers could enjoy lemons, oranges, fruit jellies, jams, pastries and sorbets.

During Apartment Evenings held three times a week **Diana Salon** served as a billiards room. Louis XIV was a good player and games were played on a crimson velvet gold-fringed table. Carpeted galleries lined the walls from which ladies of the court watched. On these evenings courtiers moved through to **Mars Salon** where musicians played from the galleries on either side of the fireplace.

The **Mercury Salon** beyond, was the original state bedchamber of Louis XIV and after his death he lay in state, attended by relays of clerics who celebrated four Masses simultaneously from dawn until midday for a whole week.

The **Apollo Salon** was his throne room and the most lavish of the suite. Here, beneath the **La Fosse** ceiling *Apollo in his Chariot accompanied by the Four Seasons* he granted audience to ambassadors.

Next are the three best-known rooms. The ceiling of the **War Salon** says it all. The central panel depicts *France Triumphant*. Side panels show Austria on her knees with the eagle at her side, Holland lying exhausted on the lion of Flanders and a defeated Spain, her lion alongside.

Through this salon and into **Hall of Mirrors**. Until 1678 this was just a terrace. At Versailles, as in English country houses, there was a need for a covered gallery in which to walk and exercise in winter. Seventeen huge mirrors reflect the light from matching windows opposite, with spectacular views over the gardens.

Above the mirrored wall is a plaque with the words *1662 order re-established in the finances* which the young Louis XIV placed there to mark the imprisonment of his ostentatious minister Fouquet.

At the far end is **Peace Salon** used by the queen as her gaming room and by Marie-Antoinette as the setting for her small theatre. The salon became part of the **Queen's Apartments** and it was in the **Queen's Bedchamber** next door that nineteen 'Children of

Hameau: a little patch of Normandy

France' were born, all in public. Only the boys were possible heirs to the throne.

Adjoining is the **Salon of the Queen's Nobles** - a title which did not imply the freedom for the Queen that her husband enjoyed in the opposite wing. Here the Queen received ambassadors.

Although many of these rooms have been restored to look exactly as they did in the 18th century there is little of the original furniture in the palace. The starry-eyed politics of the infant republic did not inspire economic confidence among its European neighbours so the State had to sell off many of the pieces and these can be seen in museums and collections throughout the world, including the Metropolitan Museum in New York; Windsor Castle; the Hermitage, Leningrad; and the Wallace Collection, London.

The next room is an **Ante-Chamber** with a family painting by **Madame Vigée-Lebrun**. This is where Louis XVI and Marie-Antoinette had their meals in public. The final room is the **Guard Room** where the Queen's Guard fought to protect her from revolutionaries.

Leave the Royal Apartments and enter the **Coronation Room** and then the south wing, the first floor of which is the **Hall of Battles**. Re-live thirteen centuries of French military victories, from Tolbiac in the 5th to Wagram, last of Napoleon's successes.

LUNCH: Cross the Royal Court-yard towards the chapel and through the gates. On the other side of the road is the Brasserie du Musée at 2, Place Gambetta run by Jean Gaidou. Being the nearest to the palace grounds it may be crowded. Service, though, is quick and cheerful. There are four set menus and a good à la carte. Alternatively, stay on the palace side of Rue des Réservoirs and, before the main crossroads, turn left towards the Bassin de Neptune where there are three other good smaller restaurants.

After lunch, into the gardens of the palace to **Bassin de Neptune**. To appreciate the finest of French landscaping techniques, walk the 800 metres of Water Avenue back to the palace, across the **Parterres d'eau** and **Parterres du Midi** to the balustrade at the **Orangery**.

Turn right, through the Queen's Grove, past the Winter Fountain to the **Apollo Fountain**, with the Sun God emerging from the sea at dawn in his chariot drawn by four spirited steeds.

Beyond is the **Grand Canal** on

which gondolas, model warships and pleasure boats sailed during the heyday of the court. Take the motor launch which weaves its way between the none-too-expert oarsmen to the Trianons. The launch fare repays in time and effort.

The Trianons Grand and Petit were small guest-châteaux. Louis XIV built the **Grand Trianon** for Madame de Maintenon, his second wife. Napoleon lived there while scheming to restore the palace as his own residence. General de Gaulle had it restored and refurnished in the sixties as a setting for State receptions.

Three hundred metres away is the **Petit Trianon** built by Gabriel. The inspiration for it was that of Madame de Pompadour, but it was first occupied by Madame du Barry. Marie-Antoinette transformed the gardens surrounding Petit Trianon from the French pattern to English style. She also built the tiny **Théâtre**, for she loved acting, and **Hameau**, a little Normandy-style village of twelve houses of which ten still remain. Walk back past the **Temple of Love** and the **Belvedere** to the canal. Take the motor launch or the stagecoach to return to the **Apollo Fountain**.

TEA: **Facing the château, walk diagonally across to the left past l'Étoile to the gate and into Avenue de Trianon. Cross to Boulevard de la Reine and Hôtel Palais Trianon, a country house hotel with traditional teas and silver trays of pastries.**

Retrace the route to the station and the return journey to the city.

DINNER: **An evening cruise along the Seine matches the spectacle of a day at Versailles. Cruise boats leave from the Bateaux-Mouches landing stage at Pont de l'Alma to follow the left bank upstream round the islands and downstream as far as the Statue de la Liberté.**

As landmarks go by they can be tracked on the special map presented with the menu. Reasonably formal dress is

---

Métro *magnifique*

The métro is the finest underground in the world - particularly for visitors. Station entrances with distinctive métro signs are always in sight in the centre and trains run from 05.30 to 00.30 every two to ten minutes. The fifteen lines are numbered and colour coded. To make the system easy to use:

Memorize the destination and name of the end-of-line terminus in that direction.

When changing trains, follow the *correspondance* signs linked with the name of the end-of-line terminus.

There are information screens on platforms and, at station exits, large-scale maps of local streets.

Buy a five-day *Paris Visite* ticket in main métro stations which buys all city travel and many attractive discounts. Also pick up the useful free booklet *Paris Patchwork*.

Passes can also be used for buses, a pleasant way to see the city if only the network of fifty-six routes were easier to understand and traffic did not make journey times uncertain.   ❏

---

expected if only to add to the romantic mood of candlelit tables and music. Dinner is a four-course 'gastronomic' menu of tried and trusted dishes, prepared on board, served with sparkling Blanquette de Limoux and red St-Émilion. There is kir and a taster to start and plenty of choice of first and main courses. Begin with pâté de foie gras on brioche, followed by sole Normande, a cheese board of brie, roquefort and comté and a dessert of omelette norvégienne, with ice cream, flamed in brandy.   ❏

Images of protest

Walking the boulevards and sitting in the haunts of Hemingway and Scott Fitzgerald, lunching at Le Procope and strolling through the playground of the Left Bank

The Left Bank is the most evocative district of Paris. The name alone conjures up images of artists and writers drinking in the boulevard cafés between the wars; Allen Ginsberg and his Beat Generation in post-war years; or, more dramatically, students in 1968 ripping up the cobblestones to fight the riot police and setting off the resignation of President de Gaulle.

The Left Bank is now calm but still fascinating. Today's tour starts near **Davioud's** intricate Second Empire fountain in the **Place St-Michel**, the meeting place for the university district of the Sorbonne, the Latin Quarter and the Left Bank.

Until the end of the 18th century only Latin was spoken in this scholars' quarter. Now the international language of tourism is the one used.

Emerge from the métro *St-Michel* into the square of old Parisian houses, now cafés with terraces spilling onto the pavements. Face away from the river and cross to the right of the fountain, past the plaque marking the pitched battle between students and German troops in 1944.

Take the road to the right of **Café Gentilhomme** the one-time haunt of Jack Kerouac and turn right into **Rue Git-le-Coeur**. Half-way down on the right is the 15th century Hôtel du Vieux Paris, restored as it was when Ginsberg and his followers used it as a base.

Out onto the **Quai des Grands Augustins**, cross at the

Les Deux Magots

Oscar Wilde

St. Sulpice

Tour Montparnasse

Cimetière du Montparnasse

Palais & Jardi du Luxembourg

lights and turn right to browse along the *bouquinistes*, traditional bookstalls which line the Seine.

Continue along Quai St-Michel until the bridge Petit Pont, cross into Rue Saint-Jacques and left into Rue de la Bûcherie.

COFFEE: On the corner is the café named after the bridge. It is an ideal location for people-watching, coffee and substantial baguettes. Opposite is the little Rue de la Huchette which, 500 years ago, was called Rue de Rôtisseurs, street of roasters, but now is dominated by Greek restaurants cooking kebabs on the spit rather than roasting whole sheep. For a more tranquil view, look across at Notre-Dame. This is one of the best vantage points to see this magnificent cathedral.

Follow the footpath in front of the café towards Square Viviani. A short way along, set back, is the English bookshop **Shakespeare & Company**. Outside is a blackboard with events and 'To Let' advertisements for apartments in London as well as Paris. Inside, owner George Whitman sits at a table surrounded by customers, many expatriates, all browsing among the thousands of English-language books, some signed by famous writer-friends.

Further on, in the square, among the lime trees, is a now propped-up *Robinia acacia*, planted in 1601 and one of the oldest trees in Paris. It was introduced from America by the botanist Robin from whom it took its name.

Tucked away in the corner is the small picturesque church of **St-Julien-le-Pauvre**, now a Greek Catholic church. For several centuries, students at the Sorbonne met here for assemblies but, ahead of their time, vandalized it and in 1524 were banned. It is still worth looking inside - past the well-head at the entrance - to admire the upper part of the two chancel pillars carved with 53

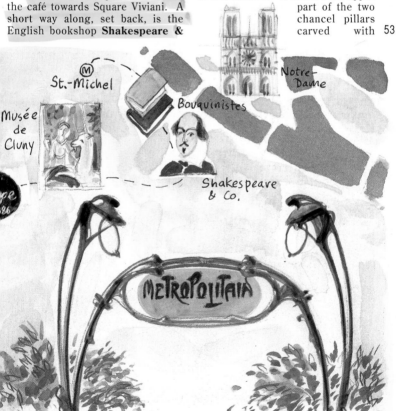

acanthus leaves. From the church, take Rue Dante into the Boulevard Saint-Germain, turn left and right into Rue de Cluny which leads to Place Paul-Painlevé and **Musée de Cluny**. The museum is in the medieval house of the Benedictine abbots of Cluny which adjoins the ruins of the Palais des Thermes, the Roman baths of the 2nd century.

Entrance to the museum is from the courtyard. Inside is a stunning **Collection of Tapestries** woven in Flanders in the 15th and 16th centuries. On the first floor, in the rotunda of room XI, are the most famous works: the set of six known as *The Lady with the Unicorn*, each panel with exquisite tiny flowers, birds and animals. In room IV, almost equally well-known, is *La Vie Seigneuriale*, tapestries describing five scenes from a nobleman's household.

On the same floor is the monk's tiny Flamboyant Gothic chapel with its one slender column and walls lined with tapestries telling *La Légende de Saint-Étienne* in twenty-three beautifully-woven scenes.

On leaving, turn right into Boulevard St-Michel, right and left into Boulevard Saint-Germain.

LUNCH: **Walk across the boulevard and, on the far side,**

Le Procope: good news

take the fourth turning on the right, the Rue de l'Ancienne-Comédie. A little way down on the right is Le Procope, founded in 1686, allegedly the oldest café in the world with a customer list that has included Voltaire, Balzac and Hugo. If there is a wait, take consolation in studying the array of world

54

Bouquinistes: for browsing along the Seine

'The Lady with the Unicorn': exquisite detail

newspapers, constant news agency reports and pictures. Food is good, service erratic although both will be forgotten when the unique atmosphere will long be remembered.

At the junction Carrefour de Buci, take **Rue de Buci** on the left. This is the area of markets by day, restaurants and jazz cellars by night. Weave between the stalls of fruit, vegetables, sea food, hot baguettes and crêpes.

Take the **Rue de Seine** on the right. Halfway along, in a side-street on the right, is a wrought-iron sculpture with its intertwining symbols of the neighbourhood's arts, books and music. On the left is Rue Visconti, tall 17th century houses on both sides, where Balzac once had a printing press.

Further along, next door to the tobacconist, is the apartment house at No 21 where George Sand lived.

Turn left into **Rue des Beaux-Arts,** typical of these traditional streets, filled with art galleries and antiquarian dealers. It has been home to poet Gérard de Nerval, painter Corot and, at No 8, the studio of Fantin-Latour. The first ten even numbers mark the site of

the palace where Queen Margot, Henry IV's first wife, lived until her death in 1615.

On the odd numbers side at No 13 is L'Hôtel. In 1870 this was the Hôtel d'Alsace and, as the plaque records, Oscar Wilde died here in 1900. His reported comment was, 'I am dying beyond my means'. The rate for the room named after him in this now luxury hotel complete with restored Mistinguett furniture, bears out his misgivings.

Turn left into **Rue Bonaparte**, the nearest any street in Paris gets to being named after Napoleon, with antique shops mingling with the courtyards of the 16th century mansions. Cross Rue Jacob where at No 53 the Treaty of Independence between Britain and America was signed by Benjamin Franklin.

On the corner with Boulevard Saint-Germain is the legendary **Café des Deux Magots**, the birth-place of Surrealism. It is still the favourite of writers and each year stages the city's book awards.

Turn left at the church and cross the boulevard at the *Mabillon* métro station into Rue du Four. Take the second turning left, the almost hidden Rue Princesse. At No 6 is the American bookshop

55

Village Voice, well-stocked and with emphasis on contemporary American literature.

Continue towards the church, past the elegant Yves Saint Laurent Rive Gauche boutique on the corner with Rue des Canettes.

The church of **St-Sulpice** is the largest church in Paris after Notre-Dame. On each side of the entrance to the impressive nave are giant shells mounted on marble rocks sculpted by **Pigalle** which were given to François I by the Republic of Venice.

In the first chapel to the right is **Eugène Delacroix's** mural *Jacob's Fight with the Angel* and in the Lady Chapel at the far end, above the altar, is **Pigalle's** *Virgin and Child*. Pride of the church is the organ above the entrance, in its splendid **Chalgrin** loft, considered one of the finest in France.

Outside, head up the hill by Rue Bonaparte to **Jardin du Luxembourg**, the playground of the Left Bank. Here are tennis courts, pony rides, *boules*, chess, a marionette theatre, ice creams and an open-air café. There is no sitting on the grass - only in designated areas for families with young children - but chairs are provided.

Luxembourg owes more to Italy than France. Marie de Médicis, homesick after the assassination of husband Henri IV, modelled the **Palais du Luxembourg** on the Pitti Palace in her native city of Florence. The **Médicis Fountain**, hidden among the greenery at the palace end of an oblong pool, is in Italian style by Salomon de Brosse.

In the early 19th century the architect Chalgrin remodelled the palace for Napoleon to house the Senate. The palace next door **Petit-Luxembourg** is the home of the President of the Senate. Scattered over the park are statues of authors and poets such as George Sand, Paul Verlaine, Stendhal and Flaubert. In front of the palace is the giant pool with fountains where children sail their model boats.

Walk away from the palace by the long garden which leads to the Paris Observatory. Cross Place A Honnorat into the **Avenue de**

l'Observatoire and continue under the trees watching the dome of the Observatory growing larger.

The Observatory set the zero meridian for France along the north-south axis of the building on the day of the summer solstice in 1667. It is just over two degrees east of Greenwich, the international meridian, which was set in 1884. It is the oldest observatory in use.

The gardens end at Davioud's extravagant *Fountain of the Four Parts of the World* with its four maidens sculpted by **Carpeaux** and eight horses by **Frémiet**.

Further on, to the right, is **François Rude's** statue of Marshall Ney, executed here in 1815 for supporting Napoleon.

TEA: Across to the right behind conifers is La Closerie des Lilas where Hemingway wrote, Lenin plotted and intellectuals of Paris still meet. Art posters for local exhibitions cover the walls and the brasserie atmosphere is relaxed and authentic. Try the tarte tatin with coffee or a glass of Saumur Champigny with an omelette. Alternatively, turn right along Boulevard du Montparnasse to its junction with Boulevard Raspail to La Coupole, the city's largest brasserie, where Josephine Baker introduced her lion cub.

Continue along Boulevard du Montparnasse to Boulevard Raspail. This was the centre of the area which once replaced Montmartre as the main Bohemian and artistic district. At La Rotonde and across the road at Le Dôme, Chagall and Matisse, Scott Fitzgerald and Cocteau used to meet. Musicians, poets and intellectuals crowded these cafés in the heyday of the twenties and thirties.

Cross the road and walk along Boulevard Raspail to its junction with Boulevard Edgar-Quinet and into the corner entrance of the **Montparnasse Cemetery**. Guy de Maupassant, J K Huysmans, Rude and Baudelaire are all buried here.

Even in the cemetery, there is still *joie de vivre*. Just inside the

56

Café des Deux Magots: dining on the boulevard

gate, turn to the left and in area 22 is an ornate double bed. Sleeping on the left side, in her street clothes is Madame Pigeon while her husband, in similar clothing, pen in hand, surveys passers-by.

In the middle of the cemetery is the grave of actress Jean Seberg, area 13, and Constantin Brancusi, marked by his fine sculpture *Le Baiser*, area 18. The shared grave of Jean-Paul Sartre and Simone de Beauvoir is just left of the main gate, area 20.

On leaving, head for the **Tour Montparnasse** which, to the anger of Parisians, dominates the skyline. At a height of 209 metres, it is the tallest office building in Europe. Below ground, there are six floors with squash courts, swimming pools and eighty shops and department stores including Galeries Lafayette.

On the approach to the tower, in Place du 18 Juin 1940 - the date de Gaulle began broadcasting from London - a plaque marks where Leclerc received the surrender of von Choltitz, the German general for Paris, on 25 August 1944.

Signs show the way to the entrance to the tower and ticket desk for the elevators to the 56th floor. If thirsty, better value is to take the free lift to the bar and restaurant. There is an open terrace at rooftop level. In the viewing-

gallery, a luminous frieze round the top of the wall picks out landmarks. After dark, the city is floodlit and buildings can be identified - Eiffel Tower, École Militaire, Notre-Dame, Palais de Chaillot, Arc de Triomphe, the Louvre, Hôtel de Ville, Panthéon and Sacré-Coeur.

This is the *ville lumière* - an extravagant spectacle to end *Seven Days in Paris*.

DINNER: After today's literary tour, dinner is on Boulevard St-Germain. Take the métro to St-Germain-des-Prés and choose from the famous: Café des Deux Magots, Brasserie Lipp or Café de Flore. At Lipp, no bookings are taken and, as an out-of-town visitor, do not expect a table in the rooms near the entrance which are for regulars and celebrities. The Alsace-style food is excellent. Alternatively, walk a short way along the Boulevard in the direction of Odéon, turn left into Rue Grégoire-de-Tours and at No 6 is Le Gregory. Bustling bistro atmosphere and traditional French dishes of quality. The gastronomique set-price menu includes half a bottle of good wine and the excellent service. Enjoy a free glass of kir if there is a wait for a table. ❑

57

Staying awhile

**For those with days to spare, a chance to explore
the City of Science, visit museums, escape to the parks
or spend an evening at the movies and on to late-night jazz**

Bagatelle, Parc du   **métro Port Maillot**
Bois de Boulogne

08.30-19.30

The Bagatelle is a park within a park, created in the Bois de Boulogne. It is renowned for its rose gardens - 10,000 plants in 1,200 varieties. There are also beautiful irises in a walled garden, peonies, clematis and water lilies as well as waterfalls and fascinating follies hidden in trees. Painting exhibitions are held regularly in the Orangerie and Trianon.

Bois de Boulogne   **métro Port Dauphine**

Once a royal forest, it is now a recreation area similar to Hyde Park or Central Park. Within Pré Catelan is Jardin Shakespeare which features plants known to and written about by the bard. His works are performed here in English at the outdoor theatre during the summer. Children will enjoy Jardin d'Acclimatation with a zoo, go-cart track and merry-go-rounds. On Sundays, racegoers converge on Longchamp and Auteuil tracks.

58

Bourse   **métro Bourse**
Place de la Bourse

12.30-14.30 closed Saturday Sunday

The tranquil appearance of the Greek-Roman temple that houses the Stock Exchange and the soothing explanatory video that welcomes visitors contrasts with the bedlam of unruly brokers in the main dealing room - soon to be stilled by computer-dealing. Buying and selling shares can be watched from the gallery.

Canal cruises   **métro Bastille**
Canal Saint Martin
Port de l'Arsenal, south of Place de la Bastille

The canal trip to Parc de la Villette takes three hours. It begins in the dimness of the tunnel passing under Place de la Bastille, but soon emerges to cruise past warehouses, tree-lined banks, quaint locks and swing bridges. Shorter trips can be taken from Quai de la Loire in Bassin de la Villette (métro *Jaurès*). Bookings for both: Canauxrama 42 39 15 00. Or take a boat at Musée d'Orsay to cruise along the Seine until connecting with canal Saint Martin just past the Ile St-Louis. Bookings Quiztour 42 40 96 97.

Catacombs   **métro Denfert-Rochereau**
1 Place Denfert-Rochereau

14.00-16.00 Tues-Fri 09.00-11.00 14.00-16.00 Sat-Sun closed Monday

Six million skeletons, retrieved from the cemeteries after a clean-out at the end of the 19th century, line the tunnels of these old stone quarries. The tour is as popular now as it was in those days when court ladies attended parties given there by the Comte d'Artois, later Charles X.

The Bagatelle: roses in the Bois de Boulogne

Cinemas

The French treat cinema seriously and almost one in four of the 400 cinemas in Paris show English-language films. Look in the events magazine *Pariscope* at the end of the movies listings for 'VO' *(version originale)* which means no dubbing. Usherettes expect to be tipped. Sample cinemas: Gaumont les Halles on the third floor of Les Halles, six first-run movies; Marignan-Concorde Pathé, Avenue des Champs-Élysées, seven first release films; and Action Écoles, 23 Rue des Écoles (métro *Maubert-Mutualité*) with an English-language festival (Woody Allen, etc) every week. See also **Pagoda Cinema**.

Égouts (sewers)   métro Alma-Marceau
Corner of Quai d'Orsay and Pont de l'Alma
14.00-17.00 Mon, Wed and last Sat of month

For the authentic smells of Paris, a brief tour through a section of the sewer network which has been sanitized for viewing. To start, there is an exhibition on the history of the sewers and a video on how the system works.

Invalides   métro La Tour-Maubourg

Hôtel des Invalides once housed nearly 6,000 old soldiers, now the number is seventy. It also accommodates four museums all with a 'war' theme. One ticket covers the first three:

Musée de l'Armée
10.00-18.00 April-September 10.00-17.00 October-March
This is a vast display, in two sections, of the art in fighting wars. The first tells the story of the French Army, through pictures, models and mementoes, particularly battles connected with Napoleon I. The second covers the first and second world wars with displays of uniforms of France and its allies.

Musée des Plans-Reliefs
10.00-17.45 April-September
10.00-16.45 October-March
In 1668 when France's army dominated Europe, Louis XIV's Secretary of State for War Louvois and military architect Vauban began the tradition of making precise 1:600 scale models of the country's fortified border towns and ports. For years these drawings were marked top secret, now they are on show.

Musée des Deux Guerres Mondiales
10.00-18.00 April-September closed Sunday Monday
10.00-17.00 October-March closed Sunday Monday
The first and second world war remembered in posters, documents and weapons. There is particular emphasis on the occupation and the French resistance, also the liberation including a scale model of the Normandy landings.

Musée de l'Ordre de la Libération
Entrance in the Boulevard de la Tour Maubourg
14.00-17.00 closed Sunday
General de Gaulle created the Order of Liberation to honour those who gave outstanding service in the freeing of France. The themes of Resistance, Deportation, Free French and Liberation are chronicled in photographs, documents and mementoes.

Jazz

Paris is jazz as far as Europe is concerned. Quality varies. Study *Pariscope* or music magazines for listings. Here are just four:

Caveau de la Huchette
5 Rue de la Huchette
The cellar and secret passages where freemasons met in the 18th century now echo each night to jazz, often Dixieland. This is the best club on the Left Bank. A different band every night and dancing until 02.30, later on Saturdays. Métro *St-Michel*.

Le Bilboquet
13 Rue St-Benoît
Well established bar-restaurant with live jazz and blues every night. The best of local groups. Métro *St-Germain-des-Prés*.

Slow Club
130 Rue de Rivoli
Favours New Orleans and Dixieland, 22.00 to 03.00, later at weekends. Claude Luter, one of the legends of Paris jazz, leads the resident sextet. Star name visitors. Closed Sunday and Monday. Métro *Louvre*.

Théâtre Dunois
112-118 Rue du Chevaleret
Now at a new address with more room. Out of the Left Bank. Wine and beer bars with food at the side of the hall. Improvized jazz, often with big bands. Métro *Chevaleret*.

Mouffetard, Rue   métro Monge
Josephine Baker and Ernest Hemingway shopped in this cobbled shopping area and at the outdoor market in Place Monge (Wednesday, Friday and Sunday) where its fresh fruit, vegetables, fish and meat stalls are famous. Less attractive are the stalls of cheap jewellery and leather goods.

Musée des Arts Décoratifs   **métro Palais Royal**
107 Rue de Rivoli

12.30-18.00 Sunday 11.00-18.00 closed Monday Tuesday

The Marsan Pavilion of the Louvre houses this museum set out in a series of rooms showing furnished interiors of a French home from the middle ages to the 20th century. It is a potpourri of medieval carvings, tapestries, 17th century marquetry furniture, Vincennes porcelain of the 18th century and 20th century Art Nouveau. A recent acquisition of a fascinating and large collection of toys adds a homely touch.

Musée de la Chasse: hunting scene

Musée de la Chasse   **métro Rambuteau**
Hôtel Guénégaud
60 Rue des Archives

10.00-12.30 13.30-17.30 closed Tuesday

Everything to do with hunting is here in one of the Marais' most beautiful houses. On the ground floor are collections of antique arms and trophies among paintings by Bruegel, Cranach, Rubens and Tiepolo. On the first floor, hunting weapons from the 16th to 19th centuries and, on the second, hunting scenes by Chardin, Oudry, Claude Monet and Desportes.

Musée Jacquemart-André   **métro Miromesnil**
158 Boulevard Haussmann

13.30-17.30 closed Monday Tuesday

Discerning collectors Edouard André and his wife Nélie Jacquemart left this mansion and their collection to the Institut de France. Its opulent interior provides a fine setting for the Italian Renaissance art - sculptures by Donatello and paintings by Botticelli, Titian and Ucello, particularly his magnificent *St George Slaying the Dragon.*

French 18th century is represented by Watteau, Fragonard, Greuze and Boucher; foreign schools by Reynolds, Murillo and Rembrandt. Adding to the elegance are Gobelins tapestries depicting the seasons, a Savonnerie carpet, Limoges enamels and Palissy ceramics.

Musée Kwok On   métro St-Paul
41 Rue des Francs-Bourgeois
10.00-17.30 closed Saturday Sunday

In the heart of the Marais is this Oriental theatre museum. Its benefactor, a wealthy Hong Kong businessman, was enthusiastic about the opera and on show among the Oriental masks, puppets, paintings and engravings are costumes and instruments from the Peking Opera and other Asian theatres.

Musée Nissim de Camondo   métro Monceau
63 Rue de Monceau
10.00-12.00 14.00-17.00 closed Monday Tuesday

The Camondo banking family left this 1914 mansion modelled on the Petit Trianon at Versailles to the State in 1917. It re-creates an aristocratic home in Louis XVI's time. *Objets d'art* include Aubusson tapestries, Savonnerie carpets, eight sketches by Oudry for Louis XV hunting scenes tapestries, paintings by Guardi and furniture by Riesener, Sené, Carlin and Oeben.

Musée de la Poste   métro Pasteur
34 Boulevard de Vaugirard
10.00-17.00 closed Sunday

Buy a sheet of stamps straight from the printing press at this fascinating postal museum. The history of these miniature works of art and the delivery services that send them on their way is told on four floors, illustrated with postmen's uniforms, mailboxes and modern sorting machines.

62

Opéra   métro Opéra
Place de l'Opéra
Rudolph Nureyev as director for the French National Ballet has brought back the international stars and the glitter to l'Opéra, now free of the opera productions which have gone to Opéra Bastille. Obtaining tickets to see the multi-national company of 152 dancers is difficult for visitors, but try the theatre box office, open 11.00 to 20.00 (47 42 57 50) or hotel reception.

Pagoda Cinema   métro Sèvres Babylone
57 Bis, Rue de Babylone
The most beautiful cinema in Paris - in a Chinese pagoda surrounded by a Japanese garden. This unlikely combination began as an indulgence at the turn of the century for the wife of the director of the Bon Marché store. Films are watched in the Grande Salle as Chinese and Japanese warriors battle it out in the ceiling painting overhead. English and American films are never dubbed. Tea and cakes can be enjoyed in the garden - until 22.00.

Palais de Chaillot   métro Trocadéro
Place Trocadéro
Four museums, an aquarium and a cinema are in the palace:
Musée de l'Homme
09.45-17.15 closed Tuesday
Traces the evolution of man from the Palaeolithic to the present day: among the most interesting artifacts are the famous *Venus of Lespugue* made from a mammoth tusk, the most important European collection of African and Oceanic art, colourful costumes from the Far East and a gallery showing musical instruments from all over the world.

L'Opéra: spotlight on the stars of the ballet

Musée du Cinéma
10.00, 11.00, 14.00, 15.00 and 16.00 closed Tuesday.
Restricted to conducted tours (in English), a demand of the founder
Henri Langlois. They are excellent and last just over an hour. The
journey to the make-believe world of film production starts with the
pioneers of cinematography, through to the 'talkies' and James Bond.
Each stage is illustrated with costumes and props such as the tunic
worn by Rudolph Valentino in *The Sheik*, the swimsuit of Esther
Williams and the head of Norman Bates' mother in *Psycho*, sent by
Alfred Hitchcock himself.

Musée des Monuments Français
09.00-18.00 closed Tuesday
Reproductions of sculpture from all regions of France, models of

Night time in Paris: cinemas, theatres and clubs

buildings and copies of mural paintings make up this collection. The plaster copies are carefully coloured to represent the original wood, marble or bronze. Travel from the cathedral of Reims to Abbey of Moissac, all in a few steps.

64

Musée de la Marine
10.00-18.00 closed Tuesday
The story of the French navy through paintings, figureheads, models and cannons. Stand on the bridge of a modern warship or imagine a trip in Napoleon's barge.

Parc de la Villette   métro Porte de la Villette

Once a cattle market and abattoir, now an exciting showcase for technology:

Cité des Sciences et de l'Industrie
10.00-18.00 closed Monday
In a futuristic setting of glass and steel with platforms and walkways linked by escalator, discover how things work with interactive computers, lasers, videos and mathematical games.
Three million visitors a year press buttons and keys and become involved in the displays. A newsroom of journalists interpret scientific news and screen the results or debate with studio audiences.

La Géode
10.00-21.00 Wed, Fri, Sat and Sun
10.00-18.00 Tues and Thurs closed Monday
This enormous sphere of mirrored stainless steel reflecting aspects of the park, houses an auditorium in which films are projected onto a huge semi-circular screen that gives the visitor the impression of being enveloped in the image. The commentary is in French but this is no problem: the images and sound effects are sensational.

Cité de la Musique
Museum of instruments, concert hall and the relocated Conservatoire National de Musique.

Inventorium
Visits every 90 minutes 11.00-15.30 Tues, Thurs and Fri
12.30-1700 Wed, Sat and Sun closed Monday
One exhibition for three to six-year-old children and another for six
to twelves. Technology is explained by games and touch, there is
even a real stream running through the younger children's section.

Zenith
Pop and rock music auditorium.

St-Eustache   **métro Les Halles**
2 Rue du Jour
09.00-19.00
The modern-day Forum des Halles next door only emphasises the beauty of
this Gothic/Renaissance church. The interior of St-Eustache is vast - soaring
34 metres in height. The glorious stained glass windows are from a sketch
by Philippe de Champaigne (1631) depicting *St Eustache with the Apostles*.
The church has an eight-thousand-pipe organ and a well-deserved reputation
for the quality of its concerts. The first performance of Berlioz's *Te Deum*
was heard here in 1855 as was Liszt's *Grand Mass* in 1866.

St-Roch   **métro Pyramides**
296 Rue St-Honoré
08.00-19.00
Although the first stone of this church was laid by Louis XIV in 1653, building
faltered until 1719 when a donation from banker John Law provided the
money for it to be completed. Because of the time it took to build, it is a
mixture of Classical and Baroque styles with a Jesuit façade. However, it has
several interesting features including a Baroque pulpit by Challe (1752-58)
and the Lady Chapel designed by Jules Hardouin-Mansart with *The Nativity*
at the altar by the Anguier brothers. Three working organs and excellent
acoustics make it ideal for the regular concerts held here.

65

Vincennes   **métro Château-de-Vincennes**
Bois de Vincennes, centuries ago the royal hunting ground, today offers
many attractions. Hire a cycle or walk round waymarked paths. At Lac des
Minimes, with three islands, are boats for hire, a restaurant and an Oriental
temple. Lac Daumesnil has a restaurant on one of two islands, reached by a
bridge. The Buddhist Temple has the largest effigy of Buddha in Europe.

Parc Floral
09.30-17.30
Flower shows are held throughout the year in the various gardens
around the lake. These include a Four Seasons Garden and others
devoted to medicinal plants, irises and bamboo. There are also riding
stables, aquarium, children's play area and restaurant.

Parc Zoologique
09.00-17.30
France's largest zoo with 1,000 species in natural habitat including
mountain sheep roaming the central rock, seventy-two metres high.

Château de Vincennes
10.00-17.15 summer 10.00-16.15 winter
The castle has been restored to match its 17th century glory when it
was a royal residence. The medieval keep, or *donjon*, is the finest in
France. Opposite, the Sainte Chapelle contains beautiful Renaissance
stained glass windows. ❏

People and places

To really enjoy Paris needs this understanding of its buildings and history and the prominent figures and artists that created its culture

Académie Française

Often referred to as *les Immortels*, the Académie Française has been engaged from its beginning in revising the official dictionary of the French language. It was founded in 1635 by Cardinal Richelieu in an effort to extend the State's control to include the French language. The Académie meets at the Institut de France, an elegant building with a dome, founded by Cardinal Mazarin and designed by architect Le Vau. The forty members of this learned society are mostly writers, others are historians, churchmen, army officers and diplomats. New members are elected when vacancies occur and it was only in 1980 that a woman, Marguerite Yourcenar, was accepted as a member. She died in 1987 and was not replaced by a woman. At meetings they wear a green embroidered coat, a two-cornered hat, a cloak and a sword.

Arc de Triomphe de l'Étoile

The arch was created by Napoleon in 1806 to celebrate his glory and that of the *Grande Armée*. As it was far from finished when Napoleon married Marie-Louise, a trompe-l'oeil arch of triumph in canvas fixed to a wooden frame was erected so that the imperial couple could pass underneath when entering the capital. The architect, Chalgrin, died in 1811, and the work stopped when Napoleon went into exile. Under the July monarchy, the minister Thiers returned to the original plan and the decoration of the arch was allocated to different artists. In 1840, four years after the completion of the arch, it was consecrated by a ceremony in honour of the return of Napoleon's ashes, when the hearse passed under it. Under the Third

Republic, the hearses of famous men passed under the arch - the most spectacular was Victor Hugo's funeral. In 1920, the arch assumed a new significance when an unknown soldier, killed in the first world war, was buried under it. Three years later the flame of remembrance was lit which veterans revive every day.

Arc de Triomphe du Carrousel

This arch owes its name to the *carrousel* or equestrian display given there in 1662 to celebrate the birth of Louis XIV's first child. Napoleon I had long been in favour of joining the Tuileries to the Louvre and the idea of having gardens with two arches of triumph, one dedicated to peace, the other to war appealed to him. Only the latter was built, to commemorate victories of 1805. Begun in 1806 and completed in 1808, it was modelled on Septimus Severus' arch of triumph in Rome and has three arcades. The decoration was designed by Percier and Fontaine. The statues above are soldiers of the Empire and the horses on top are copies of originals which were trophies of General Bonaparte. These unfortunate horses were indeed much travelled, having been taken from the Sun Temple at Corinth to Venice by a doge, and then from San Marco to Paris in 1797. In 1815, they were returned to Venice. Perhaps because of its situation, this arch is one of the most photographed monuments in Paris.

Assemblée Nationale

Often called the Palais Bourbon, because it was originally built by the Dowager Duchess de Bourbon, on the Quai d'Orsay in 1722. In 1790, it was taken over by the State and renamed the Palais de la Révolution and under the

Directory, in 1795, became the Council of Five Hundred. Napoleon had a new façade built with Corinthian columns which echoed that of the Église de la Madeleine on the other side of Place de la Concorde. The debating chamber where the Assembly meets was built between 1828 and 1832, is shaped like a half moon and called the hemicycle. Unlike the British House of Commons, members speak from a tribune and are arranged in groups sitting from the left to the right of the President of the Assembly according to political opinions. The President, who is the third most important official in the country after the Presidents of the Republic and the Senate, has his residence in the Hôtel de Lassay next to the Assembly.

Balzac, Honoré de

1799-1850 Endowed with extraordinary energy which he stimulated with enormous quantities of coffee, he wrote some ninety novels in twenty years. His best works, *Eugénie Grandet* and *Le Père Goriot* are famous for their realism. By using some of his characters in different novels, he aimed at creating a whole, coherent world, the *Comédie Humaine*, which includes scenes of Parisian and provincial life.

His works which conjure up French society under the restoration derive their strength from a mixture of realism rooted in acute observation and of visionary power. Dogged by poverty and failure of business ventures, he died in August 1850, three months after marrying his old friend Madame Hanska.

Baudelaire, Charles

1821-1867 One of the greatest French poets, Baudelaire had an unhappy childhood traumatized by the second marriage of his widowed mother to an authoritarian officer of the French Army. In 1841 he was sent to India in order to tear him away from his Bohemian existence. Feeling homesick, he never went further than Mauritius and returned home enriched by the poetic beauty of the sea and exotic countries. He made a name for himself first as an art critic, writing about the Salon in 1845, 1846 and 1859. His collection of poems *Les Fleurs du Mal* (The Flowers of Evil) was published in 1857 and immediately banned as immoral. The title may have been provoking, but it is great poetry, written about the tragedy of man torn between his powerlessness and weakness on the one hand and aspiration to an ideal on the other.

Ill, addicted to opium and hashish, he had to work feverishly in order to pay his debts. In 1864 he went to Belgium in the hope of restoring his finances by delivering a round of lectures but was transported back to Paris in 1866 in a desperate state of health and died the following year.

Brancusi, Constantin

1876-1957 The sculptures of Brancusi who settled in Paris in 1904 were influenced by tribal African art and by peasant artefacts of his native Rumania. One of his favourite subjects was Mademoiselle Pogany whom he represented with a stylized head, a long neck and bulging eyes. On the Piazza at the Pompidou centre is a reconstruction of his studio with all the sculptures which were there at the time of his death.

Braque, Georges

1882-1963 Born in Argenteuil, a favourite haunt of the Impressionists, Braque associated with Matisse to lead the Fauve movement, the derisory name meaning 'wild beast'. From 1908 to 1914, Braque and Picasso invented Cubism, which submitted the subject matter to a geometrical pattern. It is sometimes difficult to distinguish Braque's paintings from Picasso's during this period, especially as they often chose not to sign their works. They worked in unison, even using the same browns and greys. Georges Braque used collage in most effective ways. His art never became abstract in so far as the subject matter always shows through the abstraction.

Cabaret at Moulin Rouge

The Moulin Rouge dates back to the days of Toulouse-Lautrec. Situated on the Place Blanche, a centre of attraction for tourists in quest of nightlife, it has nothing to do with the genuine windmills which were dotted on the Butte Montmartre as late as the beginning of the 19th century. Only one of those has survived, the Blutefin or Moulin de la Galette which became one of the most popular dance-halls in Paris in the late 19th century and has been much painted, in particular by August Renoir and Raoul Dufy.

Carpeaux, Jean-Baptiste

1827-1875 Carpeaux won the Prix de Rome in 1854 which enabled him to go to Italy where he much admired the Sistine Chapel of Michelangelo. His work was at first coolly received in Paris, but he had the good fortune of being supported by Napoleon III's cousin, Princess Mathilda. He was commissioned for the central group of the Pavillon de Flore at the Louvre. The statues of his *Four Parts of the World* which crown the Fountain of the Observatory and the *Dance* which adorns the façade of the Opéra confirm him as a great sculptor.

Chaillot, Palais de

Napoleon I chose what used to be the Hill of Chaillot to build this vast palace for his son and heir. His downfall cut his project short. After the 1878 exhibition, an odd Moorish palace with a rotunda and two minarets, the Trocadéro, was left and when preparations for the 1937 international exhibition began, a competition was held for the best solution to deal with this white elephant. The winner Jacques Carlu, with his two colleagues Azéma and Boileau, transformed the strange exotic place into the dignified building which still dominates the Place du Trocadéro. It is divided into two pavilions which house four museums: the Museum of Man, Marine, French Monuments and Cinema. On a lower level is a vast theatre, the Théâtre National Populaire, which reached great fame under the directorship of Jean Vilar. From the back where the two wings form a hemicycle, is a magnificent view of the gardens which slope gently down to the river, and on the left bank, to the Eiffel Tower, the Champ de Mars and the École Militaire.

Cluny, Musée de

Situated near the Sorbonne, the Cluny is interesting on three counts: for its ruins of Roman baths, its abbot's palace and the medieval museum. From the Boulevard St-Michel, ruins of the 2nd century palatial Roman baths are visible through the railings. On the Place Paul-Painlevé is the entrance to the abbot's palace built in the 15th century by the abbot of Cluny, Jacques d'Amboise. This is a mansion of particular interest as it is, with the Hôtel de Sens, the only medieval example of rich domestic architecture in Paris. It was built at the end of the medieval period and has evolved away from the traditional military style of the middle ages to become a charming residence in Flamboyant style, still untouched by the Italian influence of the Renaissance.

The palace was badly damaged under the Revolution, but Alexandre du Sommerard lovingly restored it and used it to harbour his medieval and Renaissance collection. Now the State has acquired it and turned it into a medieval museum where tapestries like the *The Lady with the Unicorn* can be admired.

Degas, Edgar

1834-1917 Born in Paris into a rich, cultured family, Degas gave up law to devote himself to painting. He spent most of his life in Montmartre and his early works reflect his Parisian interests - races at Longchamp, the orchestra of the Opéra and rehearsals of the corps de ballet. Because of the family responsibilities caused by the financial ruin of his brother, he changed his style of life, shunning society salons and dedicating

Moulin Rouge.

himself exclusively to his art. He painted Parisian men and women in their daily activities - laundresses, businessmen talking together. A great friend of Monet, Renoir and Pissaro, he proved one of the most adventurous painters of his time, allowing himself to be influenced by Japanese art, experimenting with odd angles as one would with a camera and with close-ups which were techniques foreshadowing the cinema.

Delacroix, Eugène
1798-1863 Born in Paris, Delacroix's vocation as a painter was begun by his admiration for Rubens and Veronese whose works he had seen at the Louvre. It was also influenced by Géricault, seven years his senior. The great painting of his youth is *The Massacre of Chios* based on a contemporary event, the slaughter of the Greek inhabitants of Chios island by the Turks, which reveals the influence of Géricault and Gros and Delacroix's attraction to Orientalism.
Although the painting caused consternation by its realism, it was bought by the State. To some he was reminiscent of Rembrandt, to others of Veronese. Among his greatest works are the *Death of Sardanapalus* and *Liberty Leading the People* illustrating the Revolution of 1830, both at the Louvre. In 1857 he established his

studio at 6 Place Furstenberg where there is a Delacroix museum.

Eiffel Tower
Named after its engineer, it was built for the Exposition Universelle of 1889 celebrating the first anniversary of the French Revolution. This Exposition also sought to put France on the map as a successful industrial power. Seven hundred engineers took part in a competition to raise an iron tower 300 metres high and Gustave Eiffel was the winner. His project was opposed by many conservationists, some of whom complained that the tower would conceal the beautiful building of the École Militaire. But Eiffel was enthusiastic. France, he claimed, would outdo the highest building in the world, which was in Washington, by 115 metres and it would be the only country in the world whose flag would fly from a pole that was 300 metres high. When completed, the Eiffel Tower was seen as elegant, slender and airy, and although the original intention had been to demolish it after twenty years, it engendered so much enthusiasm that it remains to this day. However, the idea that it is liable to be removed persists and, after the second world war, it was the subject of a remarkable confidence trick when a Dutch scrap metal dealer, claiming that he had bought it, sold sections to credulous speculators. The tower has been painted innumerable times and was the setting for Cocteau's play *Les mariés de la Tour Eiffel*. In the summer of 1940 those who lived near to it were puzzled by a rhythmic, clanking noise which occurred every afternoon. They discovered it was German soldiers whose first idea, when they entered Paris, was to mount to the top of the tower and, since the lifts were not working, they had to climb it on foot.

Élysée Palace
The official Parisian residence of the President of the Republic, the Palais de l'Élysée is surrounded by high walls and sentry boxes occupied by Republican Guards. Built in 1718 for the Comte d'Evreux, it became the residence of Madame de Pompadour in 1753 and, after her death, was bought by a financier and embellished by the architect Boullée. With the Revolution it was divided into apartments (the poet Alfred de Vigny, born in 1797, spent some of his childhood there) while the grounds were given over to dances and public celebrations. It then changed hands many times. Napoleon's sister, Caroline, lived there with her husband, Murat. Napoleon gave it to his wife Josephine, then bought it back after their divorce. It was there that he signed his act of abdication in June 1815, after Waterloo. Only after 1848, under Louis Bonaparte, first as President of the Republic, then as Emperor Napoleon III did the palace again become the official residence of the head of state. Not every President of the Republic has appreciated it. In 1958 General de Gaulle considered finding another residence, and would leave every week-end for his private house at Colombey-les-Deux-Églises. His three successors as President of the Fifth Republic have continued to live in their private residences. Since 1958 the President and his Cabinet meet there every Wednesday morning and afterwards, on the steps of the Élysée, the official spokesman tells the Press what has happened.

Flaubert, Gustave
1821-1880 Educated in Rouen, Flaubert shared the Romantic exaltation of his contemporaries. He went to Paris to study law and met Victor Hugo, but his stay in Paris came to an end when a nervous illness forced him to retire to his house at Croisset near Rouen where he dedicated himself to novel writing. His masterpiece is *Madame Bovary* a realistic and objective novel based on a news item in a local newspaper. Flaubert was a painstaking artist and his prose is both concise and musical. In 1880 he died suddenly, saddened

Guimard's Metro.

by several bereavements and yet cheered by the increasing influence of his works.

Gobelins
The tapestry works is named after the Gobelins family who settled in Paris in the 15th century. Two Flemish tapestry-makers took over during the reign of Henri IV. Colbert expanded the works considerably under Louis XIV when they became the *manufacture royale de tapisseries et de meubles de la Couronne* under the direction of Le Brun and later Mignard, two famous painters of Louis XIV's reign. Most of the beautiful tapestries and pieces of furniture which decorated the royal palaces were made there and all the Gobelins' production still goes to the State. Many of the tapestries are made from the designs of famous painters, like Lurçat and Picasso.

Guimard, Hector
1867-1942 An architect most representative of the 1900s style of Art Nouveau. Although he was born in Lyon, his career was fulfilled in Paris and its suburbs. It is only after staying in England and Brussels in 1895 that he developed his interest in Art Nouveau. His Castel Béranger apartment house in Paris was a striking example of this new style with its variety of materials and the harmony between its elaborate architectural design

and the fanciful ornamentation of doors and windows. He was commissioned to build the entrance to métro stations and worked at this from 1900 to 1912. They varied a great deal from the simplest ones with a balustrade and a few panels to a pavilion with glass roof as at the Bastille. The material he chose, cast iron, lent itself to graceful designs and imaginative motifs of decoration generally inspired by vegetation. He allied practicality and a feel for the functional with great aesthetic sense. It is a pity that subsequent generations, insensitive to the artistic and creative quality of his work, destroyed so much of it.

Haussmann, Baron
1809-1891 Prefect of the Seine under Napoleon III from 1853 to 1870, Haussmann, in the course of those seventeen years, transformed Paris. His plan was a capital city where carriages could circulate freely, pedestrians walk safely and railway stations, built on the periphery, would be linked to the centre by wide thoroughfares. It was most important for him, and he was fully supported by Napoleon III, that in case of revolutionary troubles, the police should be able to act efficiently, hence the straight avenues where it would be difficult to erect barricades. He was of course accused of destroying old Paris. The insalubrious districts were razed, but with them went

71

their picturesque medieval character, as was the case of the Ile de la Cité. On the other hand, he created new vistas. His straight streets are often saved from monotony by seductive prospects: along the Boulevard St-Michel, the spire of the Sainte-Chapelle appears in the distance, or the towers of Notre-Dame along the Rue Beaubourg. Paris is full of such surprises. He was the first to plant trees along streets, more than 100,000 of them. He created parks: Montsouris, les Buttes, Chaumont and he even redesigned the Bois de Boulogne.

Haute couture

The first grand couturier was Worth, an Englishman who settled in Paris at the age of twenty in 1845. Worth benefited from the industrial prosperity established by the July monarchy and established his business on a big scale in the Rue de la Paix. He fought hard to save the Lyon silk industry threatened by the increasing use of machinery. Empress Eugénie and many ladies of the Court were among his faithful customers. He dealt the final blow to cumbersome crinolines. Poiret, who achieved fame before the first world war, is remembered for his attempts to free women from their corsets and create a fluidity of style. His Oriental-inspired clothes were influenced by the Russian ballet. But the couturier who caught the imagination of the modern woman around 1925 was Coco Chanel with her comfortable and elegant clothes, shorter skirts, jersey suits and costume jewellery. Poiret and Coco Chanel were closely associated with the artistic world. The new generations of couturiers are probably less so. Most of them have had to widen the range of their customers by meeting the demands of the very rich - and these tend to be foreigners - and catering for the less wealthy by opening boutiques. The most famous couturier after the second world war was Christian Dior who launched the New Look in 1947: feminine clothes which delighted the women after years of war austerity.

Henri IV

Reigned 1589-1610. Henri IV has always been the most popular of French kings. Born in Pau, in the south, he was a leader of the Huguenots, or Protestants, during the religious wars which marked the second half of the 16th century. When he succeeded his assassinated cousin Henri III, at the age of forty-five, he had lived the wandering and dangerous life of a partisan leader. He had mixed with all sorts of people who appreciated his vitality, good humour and intelligence. Henri IV ended the religious wars in 1593 by abjuring Protestantism and, five years later with the Edict of Nantes, establishing religious freedom and toleration. Old hatreds persisted however and he was assassinated as he rode in an open carriage. He was known as good King Henri, the man who restored peace and unity to France and whose ambition was for every peasant to have 'a chicken in the cooking pot on Sundays'.

Hugo, Victor

1802-1885 One of the greatest French writers, Hugo belongs to the Romantic generation - his poetry explores great lyrical themes. His plays illustrate a new conception of the theatre, totally at odds with the rigid rules of the Classical tragedy, and the success of *Hernani* in 1830 consecrated, for a time at least, the victory of the Romantic drama over the Classical theatre. His novels *Les Misérables* and *Notre-Dame de Paris* depict the life of the socially deprived in the capital. Profoundly involved in the political life of the country, he made an enemy of Napoleon III and had to live in exile in Jersey and in Guernsey from 1851 to 1870. His return to Paris was soon followed by the disastrous siege of Paris and the Commune. In 1876, he became a member of the Upper Chamber. When he died, he was granted a national funeral and buried at the Panthéon.

d'Orsay - Home of the Impressionists.

Huysmans, Joris Karl

1848-1907 Of Dutch origin, Huysmans was born in Paris. Three stages of his novels can be detected. A follower of Émile Zola at first, he was attracted to naturalism, a form of realism which dealt mostly with the poorer section of society and the seedy side of life and wrote several documentary novels in this vein. However, a more refined side of his nature expressed itself in *À Rebours* in 1884 in which vulgar reality is rejected in a quest for an unknown universe.

After showing an interest in black magic, he discovered the beauty of Christian art. His last works *La Cathédrale* and *Les Foules de Lourdes* reveal the mystical fervour of a neophyte.

Impressionists

In 1863 Napoleon III opened the Salon des Refusés to exhibit the works of artists who had been rejected by the official Salon. Those *refusés,* Monet, Renoir, Sisley, Manet and Degas were painters who refused to submit to the conventions of academic art and to treat the historical and mythological themes favoured by traditional artists. They chose to paint what they saw around them either in the countryside or in cities. They took their easels outside and painted landscapes and allowed themselves to be influenced by Japanese prints and by the art of photography. They called themselves Impressionists after the critic Louis Leroy who had seen Monet's *Impression, Sunrise* had used the word to ridicule them. They spent weekends at Fontainebleau enjoying the beauty of the forest. In 1869 Monet and Renoir had a summer in Bougival by the river Seine where they both painted la Grenouillère, a restaurant by the river. Argenteuil was another of their favourite haunts.

Their paintings convey an idyllic vision of people picnicking and enjoying themselves against the colourful setting of forest, field and river.

If their works now fetch astronomical prices, and granted that they found admirers in their lifetime among the cultivated intelligentsia, they were never fully accepted by the official art world. At the 1900 Universal Exhibition, the Academician Jean Gérome

73

stopped the French President on the threshold of the Impressionist Room with these words: '*Arrêtez, Monsieur le Président, c'est ici le déshonneur de la France!*' 'Go no further, Monsieur le Président. This is a disgrace to France.'

Kerouac, Jack
1922-1969 An American writer of Breton-Canadian and Red Indian origins, Kerouac was born in Lowell, Massachusetts. Influenced by Hemingway, he was attracted to living in Paris and determined to establish his own style. A restless traveller and an adventurous individualist, he developed his own spontaneous prose and became the most famous of the so-called beat generation; the novel that established his reputation was *On the Road*, 1957.

Lapin Agile, Montmartre
A cabaret dating back to the late 19th century at a time when Montmartre was popular among artists and attracted many people in search of entertainment. It was called Le Rendez-vous des Voleurs. in 1880 it was redecorated and a new sign representing a rabbit clutching a bottle and jumping out of a saucepan was designed by the artist André Gil. So the name of the cabaret became Le Lapin à Gil (Gil's rabbit) and then Le Lapin Agile (the nimble rabbit). It was frequented by writers and artists. Renoir and Verlaine were amongst its customers and later Max Jacob and Apollinaire.
The cabaret had by then been bought by Aristide Bruand, one of the most famous entertainers of Montmartre with his big black hat and red scarf, and his popular songs. It was later run by Frédérick Gérard, known to all his customers as Frédé.

Legion of Honour
The National Order of the Legion of Honour was created in 1802 by the Consulate (Bonaparte) in order to reward military and civil services to the state. Those who have this honour wear red rosettes in their buttonholes. Each minister proposes names that fall within the jurisdiction of his department. There is a hierarchy of five classes: grand cross, grand officer, commander, officer and knight. It is not possible to accede to a higher rank without holding the lower one. The Palace of the Legion of Honour was built in 1784 by the architect Rousseau for the Prince de Salm, who soon after was ruined financially and guillotined in 1794. Acquired by the Chancellery of the Legion of Honour in 1804, it was destroyed by the Commune in 1871 and rebuilt by a subscription amongst the members of the Legion. An exact replica of this palace can be seen in San Francisco where it is called the Palace of the Legion of Honour.

Louvre
No building in Paris has known such changes in its fortunes. Originally a fortress built by Philippe-Auguste (reigned 1180-1223) to protect the city from invasions when he was away in the crusades, it was extended by Saint Louis (Louis IX reigned 1226-1270). Charles V (known as Charles the Wise, who reigned 1364-1380) transformed it into an elegant royal residence. It was subsequently deserted by the kings for some 150 years until François I (who reigned from 1495 to 1547) decided to live there in 1526. Most of the old building was demolished, but remains of the former structure have recently been found when new underground galleries were being rebuilt. These form the *crypte archéologique*.
François I's son, Henri II (who reigned from 1547 to 1559) pursued the completion and expansion of the palace, Henri IV built the gallery along the Seine which is called *la galerie du bord de l'eau*, or the Long Gallery, meant to join the Louvre to the Palace of the Tuileries (now destroyed) whilst Louis XIV contributed the Perrault Colonnade. Around 1678 however, Louis XIV lost all interest in the Louvre and abandoned it for Versailles. Ransacked under the Revolution, the Louvre was

Lapin Agile – Montmartre.

restored and enlarged by Napoleon. Napoleon III made certain additions (which are usually considered to be tasteless) and he decreed that the Louvre must be considered as being completed. The Louvre first became a museum under the Revolution, in 1793. It is obvious that, in spite of Napoleon III's decree, such an important monument to history and art must constantly adapt to the needs of the time.

Molière
1622-1673 A 17th century playwright, producer and actor, the son of a wealthy bourgeois, Molière devoted his life entirely to the theatre in spite of the anathema of such a profession. He is one of the great playwrights of all time. His real name was Jean Baptiste Poquelin. After touring the South of France for twelve years, he settled in Paris where his company took the name of Troupe de Monsieur, after the king's brother. The king gave him the Théâtre du Palais Royal in 1661 and supported him against his many enemies. He

died in 1673 and is remembered for his wide-ranging comedies, farces, comedies of manners and comedies of character; for making his audience laugh at the vagaries of society: title-hunting, preciosity, pedantry and snobbery; and at the vices of human beings, miserliness, greed and hypocrisy.

Notre-Dame de Paris
Built in the 12th century, its grandiose conception is associated with Bishop Maurice de Sully who wanted this to be the most beautiful church of the city. In less than a century Notre-Dame had been almost completed, which gives it a remarkable unity.
It illustrates the transition between Romanesque and Gothic architecture and makes it a pioneer amongst the great French cathedrals.
In 1793 it became the Revolution's Temple of Reason. Ironically, Robespierre saved it from destruction. In 1831 Victor Hugo stirred public opinion in favour of the cathedral's restoration with his evocative novel *Notre-Dame de*

Paris and the work was entrusted to Viollet le Duc.

Great artistic sense combines strength with elegance. The square towers are lightened with lancets and, from the top of the northern tower, is a magnificent view over the spire and the fantastic gargoyles. The interior has silence and an atmosphere of mystery.

It was at Christmas 1886 that twenty-year-old Paul Claudel entered Notre-Dame, where the choir was singing, and was converted to Catholicism. He became the leading Catholic writer of several generations.

On 26 August 1944 General de Gaulle made his triumphant march from the Arc de Triomphe to Notre-Dame. As he reached the portals, shots rang out. There was further shooting inside as the *Magnificat* was sung, but who was responsible for this fusillade has always remained a mystery.

76 **Renoir, Pierre Auguste**
1841-1919 In 1848, the family moved from Limoges, where his father was a tailor, to Paris just in time to see King Louis-Philippe and Queen Amélie leave their palace for the last time. He trained as a porcelain decorator. Finding himself without a job, he succeeded in being admitted to the École des Beaux-Arts. A stay in the forest of Fontainebleau at Barbizon with Monet and Sisley opened his eyes to the beauty of the countryside. After a time of indecision, he lightened his palette and rejected conventional themes to paint places and people as he saw them. Rheumatism which afflicted his last twenty years forced him to live in the South of France. He settled near Cagnes and went on painting using a device to fasten his brush to his hand. Renoir was the first Impressionist to make a satisfactory living by his painting.

Rodin, Auguste
1840-1917 Now considered the greatest sculptor of his time, Auguste Rodin had difficult beginnings. He failed to be admitted at the École des Beaux-Arts and became the assistant to another sculptor to make a living. In Rome, he studied the works of Donatello and Michelangelo and, after two attempts to have his work accepted for the Salon, he finally succeeded in 1879 with his *Saint Jean-Baptiste*. Among his best-known sculptures are the *Burghers of Calais*, conjuring up one of the tragic episodes of the Hundred Years' War, and a number of official monuments - Victor Hugo, a bust of Clemenceau and a full-length statue of Balzac which the Société des Gens de Lettres refused after commissioning it because it did not conform with traditional art.

Sand, George
1804-1876 This is the nom de plume of Aurore Dupin. Born in Paris, she is remembered for her novels and for the passionate life she led. Famous men succeeded each other in her life, such as the poet Alfred de Musset and the musician Chopin. Her first novels were an outlet for her romantic nature and her feminism. Later, she turned to a form of socialism which led her to take a compassionate interest in the peasants of the Berry where she lived from 1839 onwards in her country house at Nohant. She was known there as the *bonne dame de Nohant*. At the same time, she wrote novels based on her province, the most famous being *Les Maîtres Sonneurs.*

Sartre, Jean-Paul
1905-1980 Perhaps the most outstanding example of the typical French intellectual. A philosopher who taught in *lycées* and lectured in universities, a novelist, dramatist, critic, editor, political commentator and activist, he was a dominant figure in post-1945 France and remained a major figure until his death. He was associated with the philosophy of Existentialism and with an independent left wing view of society.

He made a positive contribution to intellectual life and through his persistent questioning of accepted

Shakespeare & Co.

values and assumptions he exercised a considerable influence on several generations. A prolific writer, the novel *The Diary of Antoine Roquentin*, the play *Huis Clos* and the partial autobiography are among his best works.

Shakespeare & Co
Sylvia Beach founded this bookshop cum lending library in 1919 in the Rue de l'Odéon. She was the daughter of an American minister from New Jersey and rejected the material comfort of bourgeois life in order to devote herself to the service of literature. She dealt in works in the English language, while, across the road, her lifelong friend, Adrienne Monnier, specialized in French

books. Shakespeare & Co became the meeting place of French, Irish, English and American writers such as Paul Valéry, André Gide, James Joyce - whose *Ulysses* she published - T S Eliot, Ernest Hemingway and Ezra Pound. She played an important rôle in bringing American literature to Paris and encouraged cross-fertilization between French and Anglo-American cultures. Shakespeare & Co is now off the Quai de Montebello in the Rue de la Búcherie.

Stein, Gertrude
1874-1946 Born in the United States, Gertrude Stein settled in Paris in 1903 with her brother Leo. They both collected art and

acquired some of the best work of the Cubist period which they eventually had to share when they fell out with each other. Gertrude lived with her friend Alice Toklas in the Rue de Fleurus, where she held a salon every Saturday between the two world wars. Picasso, Matisse, Braque and Juan Gris were among her frequent visitors. Ernest Hemingway became one of her *protégés* about 1922 and he introduced her to Scott and Zelda Fitzgerald. She wrote novels which she had difficulty in getting published, although they are now sought after. It has been said that she was a precursor of the *Nouveau Roman* and that she sometimes wrote like James Joyce. She certainly never liked him, probably sensing in him a rival who might keep her out of the limelight.

Toulouse-Lautrec, Henri de
1864-1901 Although born at Albi in the South of France, Toulouse-Lautrec is associated with Montmartre as his works depict the life of entertainers and customers in the cafés and cabarets. He transformed the art of poster-painting by introducing stylized human characters. Jane Avril and Aristide Bruand were painted by him repeatedly. He was influenced by Japanese prints and borrowed from these the flattened effect which sometimes led to caricature.

Utrillo, Maurice
1883-1955 Utrillo was the illegitimate son of Suzanne Valadon, also a painter. He specialized in Montmartre scenes of great charm but became an alcoholic and his mother forced him to stay at home, away from cafés, and reputedly supplied postcards of Montmartre for him to use as the starting point for his works.

van Gogh, Vincent
1853-1890 van Gogh arrived in Paris in 1886 and made friends with Toulouse-Lautrec. Under the influence of the Impressionists, he brightened his palette and painted views of Montmartre and portraits.

He then left for Provence in 1888 where he developed his own style and range of colours: Prussian blue, bright yellow, red and green. He became a friend of Gauguin in Arles, then they quarrelled. After trying to strike him, he cut his own ear off and was sent to the Arles hospital and later, at his own request, to the asylum of St Rémy. He finally settled at Auvers sur Oise, north west of Paris, under the wing of Dr Gachet who bought a number of his pictures. He shot himself in 1890, six months before his brother Theo, who had supported him all his life, died in a fit of madness. Both brothers lie next to each other in the churchyard of Auvers.

Voltaire
1694-1778 One of the most significant French philosophers of the 18th century and more particularly of the pre-revolutionary period. Imprisoned twice in the Bastille for his attacks against influential aristocrats, he found a haven in England.
Back in Paris, he made his life uncomfortable by his attack against absolute monarchy and kept running the gauntlet of arbitrary power.
He found refuge at various places: with Madame du Châtelet at her country house of Cirey; at the Court of Stanislas in Lorraine; at the Court of Frédéric of Prussia; and his last retreat, a château at Fernay, close to the frontier of Switzerland where he played host to distinguished visitors. He made a triumphal return to Paris at the age of eighty-four, but died the same year.
Voltaire touched upon all the essential problems of his time. A believer in democracy and yet not a revolutionary, he thought that enlightened monarchy was the answer and chose England as a model. His works were many and varied: tragedies in the manner of Shakespeare, pamphlets, the remarkable *Lettres Anglaises* or *Lettres Philosophiques* and many philosophical tales including *Candide*, a masterpiece. ❏

Map reading

From rue to boulevard, place to porte · this index matches each one to the large-scale pull-out map

Each name is listed in alphabetical order. A letter (or letters) and a number (or numbers) after the name are a key to its position on the map. The map is divided into sections, each marked with a letter and a number.

To help with the planning of future editions the authors would welcome comments and reactions. Please write to:

Carole and William Halden, Honeysuckle Cottage, Mill Lane, Uplyme, Lyme Regis, DT7 3TZ, England